CAMBRIDGE International Examinations

Career Award

Travel and Tourism

Standard Level

Ann Rowe, John D. Smith
and Fiona Borein

CAMBRIDGE
UNIVERSITY PRESS

PUBLISHED BY THE PRESS SYNDICATE OF THE UNIVERSITY OF CAMBRIDGE
The Pitt Building, Trumpington Street, Cambridge, United Kingdom

CAMBRIDGE UNIVERSITY PRESS
The Edinburgh Building, Cambridge CB2 2RU, UK
40 West 20th Street, New York, NY 10011–4211, USA
477 Williamstown Road, VIC 3207, Australia
Ruiz de Alarcón 13, 28014 Madrid, Spain
Dock House, The Waterfront, Cape Town 8001, South Africa

http://www.cambridge.org

First published 2002

Printed in the United Kingdom at the University Press, Cambridge

Typeface: Meridien 10/13.5pt.   *System:* QuarkXPress®

A catalogue record for this book is available from the British Library

ISBN 0 521 89235 X paperback

UNIVERSITY *of* CAMBRIDGE
Local Examinations Syndicate

Cambridge International Examinations
1 Hills Road
Cambridge
CB1 2EU
United Kingdom

Telephone: 01223 553553
Facsimile: 01223 553558
International Dialling Code: +44 1223

E-mail: international@ucles.org.uk
Website: www.cie.org.uk

29 July 2002

With Compliments

Dear Alan

I thought you would be interested to see the published version of material you reviewed earlier in the year! Thank you for all your help.

With hot wishes

Camill Elie

Contents

Introduction   1

Part 1 The Core Module

1   The travel and tourism industry   3
   - The structure of the international travel and tourism
     industry   3
   - Social, cultural, economic and environmental impacts
     of travel and tourism   15
   - Role of national governments in forming tourism policy
     and promotion   23
   - Patterns of demand for international travel and tourism   25

2   Features of worldwide destinations   31
   - The main global features   31
   - Time zones and climates   35
   - Travel and tourism destinations   40
   - What attracts tourists to a particular destination   50

3   Customer care and working procedures   64
   - Dealing with customers and colleagues   64
   - Essential personal skills required when working in travel
     and tourism   69
   - Handling enquiries, making reservations and receiving
     money   74
   - Using reference sources to obtain information   82
   - Presentation and promotion of tourist facilities   86

4   Travel and tourism products and services   88
   - Tourism products and ancillary services   88
   - The roles of tour operators and travel agents   94
   - Support facilities for travel and tourism   98
   - Worldwide transport in relation to major international
     routes   106

Part 2 The Optional Modules

5 **Marketing and promotion**   118
  - Role and function of marketing and promotion   119
  - Market segmentation and targeting   123
  - 'Product' as part of the marketing mix   124
  - 'Price' as part of the marketing mix   127
  - 'Place' as part of the marketing mix   129
  - 'Promotion' as part of the marketing mix   131

6 **Travel organisation**   135
  - Travel providers   135
  - Methods of travel   138
  - Sources of information   148
  - Ancillary travel services   152
  - Planning a travel itinerary   156

7 **Visitor services**   164
  - The role and function of tourist boards and tourist
    information centres   165
  - Provision of products and services   171
  - Marketing and promotion   173
  - Quality control   175
  - Business travel services   178
  - Leisure travel services   181

Examination techniques   184
List of useful websites   186
Glossary of terms   187
Acknowledgements   192
Index   193

Introduction

This book is designed to help you as you progress through your course. It has been written to cover all the assessment objectives, knowledge and skills criteria for the Cambridge International Examinations (CIE) Career Award in Travel and Tourism at Standard Level.

It is written in two parts: Part 1 covers all four sections of the Core Module, and Part 2 each of the Optional Modules. The book closely follows the structure of the syllabus. Each chapter in Part 1 covers a section of the Core Module, and each chapter in Part 2 one of the three Optional Modules. Activities are included throughout the chapters, which ask you to relate the theory just covered to your own locality or area. These will give you the opportunity to develop reasoning and analytical skills. Extension activities at the end of chapters give you practice in the type of activities involved in the examinations.

Certain words and terms in the text have been printed in bold type. These are terms used in the syllabus and have been highlighted to help you quickly identify these terms for reference and further development.

At the end of the book you will find a section about examination techniques to guide you further on the type and length of answer expected in the examinations. The list of useful websites includes a selection of sites containing information relevant to the travel and tourism industry. The glossary of terms will help you understand some of the terms used in the travel and tourism industry and throughout this book. It will help ensure clarity and consistency in interpretation throughout the syllabus.

The syllabus

To gain the full award, you need to complete the Core Module and two of the three Optional Modules. The Optional Module on Visitor Services is tested by assignment and all the other Modules are assessed by examination. The Core Module is tested by way of one paper lasting 2 hours 30 minutes usually consisting of four questions which address all the assessment objectives. Modules 5252 and 5253 are each tested by papers of 2 hours 30 minutes which can be attempted at the same examination session as the Core Module or on one of the alternative sessions.

These papers all contain stimulus materials taken from trade journals, real articles or promotional materials relating to actual attractions and students are expected to be able to relate their understanding of the theory to these new situations created by the stimulus materials. It has been decided not to include solutions to extension activities in this book due to the rate of change in the industry, but your teacher should be able to assess your efforts after referring to examiners' reports. The questions used for extension activities are similar to those on examination papers but usually no stimulus materials have been given.

Optional Modules can also be attempted as stand-alone examinations and certificates are issued for any module successfully achieved. However in order to achieve success in the Optional Modules, candidates would need to have sufficient underpinning knowledge contained in the Core Module.

The final Optional Module is tested by means of an assignment produced by the student, after guidance from the teacher, which clearly addresses all the assessment objectives in that module. Like the examinations, this assignment is externally marked using the criteria from the specification.

The authors of this textbook are all Principal Examiners of the Standard Level syllabus for Cambridge International Examinations and have experience teaching and examining Travel and Tourism related courses. They are also involved with the training of tutors and teachers who will deliver the courses and with the production of tutor packs and specimen materials to support the course.

Note: The terrorist attack in the USA on September 11, 2001 will affect some of the statistics and projections in this book. This highlights the volatility of the travel and tourism industry and the impact that terrorism and political unrest have on demand.

The travel and tourism industry

1

The structure of the international travel and tourism industry

We begin by looking at all the main organisations involved in the travel and tourism industry. This forms the foundation for all the other topics covered in this book and explains some of the key terms that you will need to understand.

What is travel and tourism? To use the example of the World Tourism Organisation (WTO) – affiliated to the United Nations and recognised as the leading international body on global tourism – tourism is:

> the activities of persons travelling to and staying in places outside their usual environment for not more than one consecutive year for leisure, business and other purposes.
>
> World Tourism Organisation, 1993

Therefore the people who are considered to be 'tourists', are those who are:
- away from their normal place of residence for a period of up to one year (but will return home);
- taking part in activities that would normally be associated with leisure and tourism;
- on a visit that is temporary and short term;

- not necessarily away from home overnight as they could be on a day trip or excursion;
- away from home but not necessarily on holiday, as they could be away on business.

'Travel and tourism' does not necessarily involve travelling abroad. Much tourism takes place within people's home country, on visits to attractions, city breaks, trips to business meetings, sports events or concerts, and visits to friends and relatives (abbreviated as VFR).

There are three main types of tourism: domestic tourism, incoming or inbound tourism and outbound tourism. We will look at each in turn.

Domestic tourism

This is when people take holidays, short breaks and day trips in their own country. Examples would be:
- a couple taking a weekend break in their own country;
- the supporters of a football team going to an away game featuring their local team;
- a family visiting relations in another part of the country, even if they live only a few miles away.

If we take figures from the British Tourist Authority for 2000, we find that British people made a total of 174.5 million trips within the UK, broken down as follows:
- 106 million were on holidays;
- 23.7 million were on business;
- 40.6 million were visiting friends or relatives;
- 5.1 million were for other miscellaneous reasons.

Incoming/inbound tourism

This describes people entering the country in question from their home country, so it is a type of international tourism. Examples could be:
- a party of Japanese visitors coming to Europe on a trip;
- teams from different countries entering a country for an international event, such as the Olympic Games;
- families from Pakistan entering England to visit relations.

For the UK, the British Tourist Authority statistics show that 25.2 million overseas visitors came in 2000, spending £12.6 billion in the UK.

Outbound tourism

This term applies when people travel away from their home country to visit other international countries for leisure or business. Examples of this could be:

- a family from Belgium going on holiday to Austria;
- business people from the UK travelling to America to visit a major exhibition;
- a day tripper from southern Malaysia visiting Singapore.

Using BTA figures for 1999, UK residents took 50.9 million visits abroad, of which 42.8 million were for leisure and 8 million were for business.

The following table summarises the range of reasons for travelling:

▼ Reasons for travel

LEISURE TOURISM	VISITING FRIENDS AND RELATIVES (VFR)	BUSINESS TOURISM

Holidays
Health and fitness
Sport
Education
Culture and
    religion
Social and spiritual
	Visiting elderly relatives
	Social visits to friends and relatives
	Wedding celebrations
		Business meetings
		Exhibitions and
		    trade fairs
		Conferences and
		    conventions
		Incentive travel (given
		    by businesses as
		    rewards for sales
		    or achievement in
		    that business)

Activity

Contact your national tourist board to obtain the figures for domestic tourism, inbound/incoming tourism and outbound tourism over the past few years. Using these figures, discuss the reasons for any possible changes and consider the effects on the economy of your country if tourism is increasing.

In order to assist people with their travel arrangements, there are specialist **travel service** providers. These include **travel agencies** who retail travel products direct to the individual or groups and **business travel agencies** who specialise in providing travel for the business customer or promoting conference trade. **Tour operators** provide a package for the individual and **principals** provide the basic services required by the travel and tourism industry. It is possible to divide the components of the travel and tourism industry into six key areas, as represented in Figure 1.

Figure 1 ►
Components of travel
and tourism

We will look at each of these in more detail. **Travel agents** provide a customer with advice and professional guidance on the choice of a holiday or to purchase travel products. The main aims of travel agents are:

- to sell holidays and associated products like insurance, car hire and currency exchange;
- to provide information;
- to advise clients.

To do this they also provide the additional services that are outlined in Chapter 2: 'Features of worldwide destinations'. They sell their products in the same way as other high street shops, so they advertise their products and special offers to supply customers with what they want. They act as agents for the suppliers of industry products or '**principals**' such as airlines, rail companies, hotels, ferry and cruise companies, car hire companies, tour operators, and foreign currency suppliers. They earn their income from the commission paid by these principals. They supply brochures to potential customers for them to browse through and then take bookings along with any deposits or payments. They will use computer reservations systems or viewdata systems to investigate availability and the costs of any planned journey or holiday and advise on the suitability of the accommodation or transport to meet the customers' needs.

Another type of travel agent is the **business travel agent** who specialises in arranging accommodation and transport specifically for the business traveller, whether this is to attend conferences, develop new business or visit existing or new suppliers. Agents arrange flights, transfers and accommodation suitable for the business traveller. Some large companies have their own travel agencies at their headquarters to organise the travel needs for the company. This is only beneficial when a company undertakes a large volume of business travel and tends to happen in large multi-national companies. You may also wish to refer to pages 94–8 in Chapter 4 for more detail on travel agencies.

A **tour operator** puts together holiday packages which consist of:
- travel (road, rail, sea, air)
- accommodation (hotels, guesthouses, self catering villas or apartments)
- travel services (transfers to and from the destination airport, car hire, excursions).

The package holidays offered may cover a wide range of destinations, both national and international, and can cover a variety of holidays, such as cruises, adventure, touring, winter and summer destinations. The tour operators act as the 'wholesalers' in the travel industry, as they produce a package holiday and then negotiate with travel agencies the commission they will receive to sell these to the end user, the customer.

There are two types of tour operator: the wholesale operators, who put together and operate tours only through retail travel agencies; and the direct sell operators, who market their products direct to the public (in other words they do not use travel agencies to promote their products).

Tour operators may specialise in a particular type of product – some only offer holidays within the home country, others operate only in a particular field, such as cruises, whereas others cover a wide range of holiday opportunities. Incoming tour operators or inbound handling agents specialise in tours for overseas visitors in the home country thus earning money for the national economy. Examples of worldwide tour operators are American Express and Thomas Cook, though there are others such as Kuoni and Preussag.

The tour operator will cost the package to include travel and accommodation and also produce brochures, employ and train staff (such as holiday representatives or tour directors). They undertake market research on not only the type of holiday in demand but which principals to use, and maintain their central reservations systems and customer support.

The principals within the industry, as previously mentioned, include the transport, accommodation and attraction providers. These provide the finance required to operate the product and act independently of tour operators or travel agencies, earning their income from sales, whether to individuals or tour operators. They supply the initial product, whether it is hotel accommodation, an airline, catering or an attraction.

Of the principals in the industry, **transport providers** are those operating any major form of transport. These would include the **airlines** (such as Cathay Pacific, Emirates or American Airways) providing the seats which an individual traveller, business person or tour operator may purchase. The airlines may be scheduled airlines operating to a timetable from large regional and national airports, or they may be chartered airlines. These are defined and discussed in more detail on pp. 138–9 of Chapter 6: 'Travel organisation'.

Ferry operators are another type of transport principal. Ferries provide vital links between groups of islands, or islands and a larger land mass (such as those which operate across the English Channel between the UK and Europe, or those which operate from the Greek mainland to its many islands). These services are provided for all travellers, not just tourists, but tickets are also sold to tour operators, through travel agencies or direct to the customer.

Rail companies, whether national organisations or privately owned rail companies, are also transport principals, and provide a scheduled service within the home country. Seats may be reserved by individual or business travellers either direct with the provider or through travel agencies. Tour operators may reserve seats for specific groups of travellers on a particular route. An example of this would be a tour operator booking seats on the Rocky Mountaineer, a scenic train which runs through the Canadian Rocky Mountains. Any seats not used by the tour operator would be available to the general public to purchase on an individual basis.

A tourist's choice of transport would depend on:
- price
- destination
- time – how much is available
- reason – visiting family or friends, business or leisure
- departure points – how easy it is to get there
- convenience.

In order to encourage more people to buy their holidays, many tour operators will provide flights from more accessible regional airports either direct to the final destination or to one of the major international airports which operate long-haul flights.

Many travellers wish to be independent at their destination and so require the services of **car hire principals** who provide cars of varying specifications to suit different group sizes and budgets. These may be hired independently through international chains, such as Hertz or Avis, to be available at the point of arrival for the period of the booking, or may be hired through travel agencies and tour operators. Many tour operators now promote self-drive holidays, where the flight and car hire are included but the more independent travellers buy their own accommodation in the destination country. Business travellers may also require car hire in order to visit customers in the destination country, so the business travel agency could make a booking.

Accommodation principals are those who build and staff hotels, villas, apartment resorts or holiday cottages which are available to any traveller. Some of these are major international chains such as Marriott Hotels, Holiday Inn, Comfort Inns and Hotels; others are smaller providers who may only own one or a small chain of hotels. The accommodation may be marketed individually by the provider or rooms purchased by a tour operator in order to make up a package holiday often at a special rate. The benefit to the accommodation provider of selling through a tour operator is that they have a more guaranteed occupancy rate throughout a holiday season. Otherwise they may have to spend large amounts of money on advertising in order to attract sufficient individual customers to make a profit.

Accommodation is divided into two basic categories: serviced accommodation (where meals are provided such as in hotels and guesthouses) and self-catering accommodation (such as cottages, chalets and apartments where the occupants provide their own food). Tourists can also reserve accommodation on different terms such as:
- bed and breakfast (where the price only includes the provision of bed and breakfast which may be cooked, buffet style or continental);
- half board (with bed, breakfast and either lunch or evening meal included in the price);
- full board (where accommodation and all meals are provided);
- all-inclusive (which includes accommodation, all meals, snacks and beverages for the period of the stay).

Within the tour operator's brochure, there will usually be some statement as to the accommodation and catering included in the cost. This will help the tourist to budget for the package holiday, knowing what is included and what must be paid for separately.

Figure 2 ▼
Examples of marketing
by principals

Figure 2 shows some examples of marketing by different principals in the travel and tourism industry. These are all taken from a national newspaper in the UK and are aimed at the individual traveller, rather than one who makes a booking through a travel agency.

Though accommodation is a major feature of travel and tourism, visitors require **catering facilities**, and principals within the industry include those providing a variety of outlets for food and refreshment. Whether a visitor is only away for a few hours, or for a longer holiday, food and/or drink will be required and these can be found at a variety of outlets. Airlines, ferries and rail principals will usually provide some form of catering and outlets will also be provided at airports or terminals. Visitor attractions often provide a variety of catering outlets which may include a cafeteria, self-service food selection area or a restaurant with waitress service. Even cinemas and theatres may sell snacks, ice creams or confectionery and drinks.

Major resort areas and hotels provide a wider choice of catering facilities, ranging from fast food outlets (such as Macdonalds, Wimpy, Pizza Hut and other international chains) to restaurants providing various meals from different ethnic regions (such as Indian, Chinese, French and Italian food). There could also be cafeterias where snacks and meals can be purchased plus bars and coffee shops. Even large shopping malls and sporting venues provide catering outlets for the convenience of participants and spectators.

The principals who provide **attractions** for the visitor will need to have undertaken market research to establish the need for the attraction in that particular location and its potential audience. Attractions may be purpose built, such as Disney theme parks in California, Florida or Paris, or they may be part of a nation's cultural heritage, such as the Louvre Gallery in Paris, or Sydney Opera House in Australia. They may also be created for a purpose, for example zoos, rare animal parks and sea-life centres set up to conserve and display animals and birds. Other attractions may relate to the industrial heritage or scientific development of a country. Some large companies allow visitors to tour their factories or manufacturing plants. An example of this is Cadbury World in the UK, the manufacturing base of Cadbury's chocolates, where visitors can see chocolate being made as well as be entertained with rides and purchase goods in the factory shop. Another example is the Corning Museum of Glass, outside New York in the USA, where visitors can watch glass-blowing demonstrations, see and touch examples explaining the history of glass and visit a café and factory shop.

Many newly developing countries and resorts see the need to have one or more visitor attraction in the area in order to widen their appeal and attract a larger number of tourists. Even those resorts which have previously relied on tourists who want a beach holiday, are now developing alternative attractions to offer more variety to the holiday experience.

Whatever the attraction, its aim is to appeal to as many customers as possible in order to make a profit and invest further in its development or improvement. Marketing is largely undertaken by the management of the attraction itself. It may be done in various ways – through the media (television, radio or newspapers), or by offering tour operators specific discounts to include the attraction as part of a package holiday or tour.

Activities

- Using one or two copies of your national newspaper, locate advertisements placed by as many principals in the travel and tourism industry as you can. Consider whether these advertisements are targeted at the individual or group traveller.
- Identify the main attractions in your country or area and investigate the number of visitors each has received over the past 10 years. If any of you have visited any of these attractions, present a report to your group on the type of experience you had and the most and least enjoyable aspects of your visit. Suggest any attractions or catering outlets which you consider would benefit your local area.

Tourists are generally classified in statistics according to the duration and purpose of their journey. If tourists are away from home for a day or less and do not need accommodation they are classified as **day trippers**. If the stay includes accommodation then they may be classified by their **length of stay**, such as one night or more. Length of stay statistics are often grouped into stays of one night, of between two and four nights, a week, two weeks, one month, and so on. Also visitors may be classified as to whether they are touring for **business or leisure** purposes.

These data can then be analysed to identify trends within the industry that will affect not only the marketing by the principals and tour operators, but also the economy of the country. This will be looked at in more detail later in this chapter.

Many countries with an established or significant travel and tourism industry, or those who wish to increase the national income by promoting tourism further, are likely to have a separate department of government or a public body responsible to government for this purpose. These bodies are known as **National Tourism Organisations** or NTOs.

In the UK, the NTO is the British Tourist Authority, and its mission is to build the value of inbound tourism to Britain, generating additional revenue throughout Britain, throughout the year. It operates in 27 overseas markets, working in partnership with the national tourism boards of England, Scotland, Wales and Northern Ireland, and gathers essential market intelligence for the tourism industry. It is funded by grant aid from the government's Department for Culture, Media and Sport, and has partnership support from airlines, hotels, local authorities and others to increase the marketing resources. It helps the tourism businesses reach overseas customers cost-effectively.

A typical NTO will have four main areas of responsibility:
- marketing;
- research and corporate planning (i.e. undertaking market research and deciding the policies and strategies for the organisation);
- development (looking at ways to develop tourism further, through customer care and quality assurance, liaison over training, trade relations and product development);
- finance and administration (managing its budgets, corporate press and publicity, staffing and general administration functions including information technology).

▼ Figure 3
Examples of marketing by National Tourism Organisations

13

As already mentioned, in the UK, the national tourism bodies (such as Wales Tourist Board, Scottish Tourist Board etc.) work in close partnership with the BTA (British Tourist Authority), and they in turn work closely with regional tourist boards. There are ten regional tourist boards in England who work closely with the local authorities or councils and tourism principals in order to improve the provision and promotion of tourist facilities and attractions in that region. Each local authority or town council may also have an officer responsible for the promotion of tourism within that smaller area, who will have the benefit of more specific knowledge of the needs of that smaller area. To try and make this clearer, study the following diagram and compare this with the operation of the NTO in your area.

▼ Figure 4
National Tourism
Organisation for
the UK

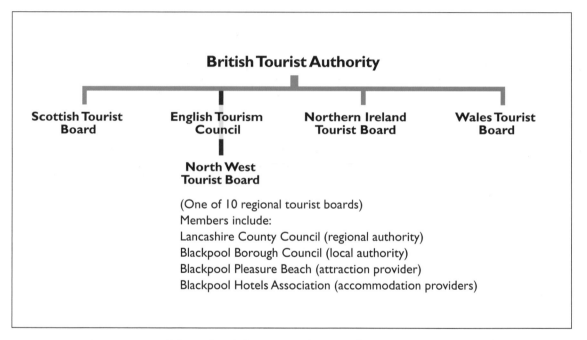

Part of the role of the regional tourist boards is to provide information to visitors when they are actually in that area. This is done through **Tourist Information Centres** (TICs). These may be located at points of entry to the areas (such as railway or bus stations) or at central points in the towns or cities, often with signs directing visitors to them. Inside the TIC there will be displays of leaflets and brochures on local attractions, entertainment venues and events, and possibly details about public transport such as timetables for buses and rail travel within the local area. There may also be a touch-screen facility enabling visitors to locate particular places of interest. One of the services provided by the TIC is information on accommodation in the area and many are able to take bookings on behalf of local hotels and guesthouses for a small deposit.

You will find more information on TICs in Chapter 6 (see pp. 149–50). You could also visit your local TIC to find out what services and information it provides to visitors.

Another ancillary service within the industry is the provision of **tourist guiding services**. These may come in the form of guides or tour directors who accompany groups of tourists round an attraction or on a specific tour provided by an operator (such as a coach tour). They are selected because of their knowledge of the specific area and also their ability to organise and manage people, so their skills must include good communication and administration. They may be required to deal with customer complaints and negotiate with other providers, such as the coach company, hotel accommodation if this is provided and excursion providers whilst on a tour.

Other types of guiding services include those specifically located at an attraction, such as museum guides. They usually have a specific, detailed knowledge of the attraction in question, and may be able to conduct tours in a particular foreign language to help visitors from overseas who do not speak the local language.

Some attraction providers now supply audio packages in various languages which can be hired by visitors for the duration of their visit. These audio tapes guide the visitor round the attraction and describe exhibits or features along the selected route. These can actually be more cost-effective for providers than employing guides, though they do lack the personal touch. Some cities also provide 'walking guides' who accompany small groups of visitors round an area, pointing out places of interest. These tend to be people local to the specific area who know it well, have been suitably trained and hold a tour guide qualification.

Social, cultural, economic and environmental impacts of travel and tourism

Social and cultural impacts of tourism

Tourism may have many different effects on the social and cultural aspects of life in a particular region or area, depending on the cultural and religious strengths of that region. The interaction between tourists and the host community can be one of the factors that may affect a community as tourists may not be sensitive to local customs, traditions and standards. The effect can be positive or negative on the host community.

Positive impacts on an area include such benefits as:

- local community can mix with people from diverse backgrounds with different lifestyles which through 'demonstration effect' may lead to the development of improved lifestyles and practices from the tourists' examples;
- there can be an improvement in local life through better local facilities and infrastructure (developed to sustain tourism) which could lead to better education, health care, employment opportunities and income;
- more cultural and social events available for local people such as entertainment, exhibitions etc.
- improved sports and leisure facilities created for the tourists which local people may use, particularly out of the tourist season;
- conservation of the local cultural heritage of an area and rebirth of its crafts, architectural traditions and ancestral heritage;
- urban areas which may be in decline can be revived and the movement of people from rural areas to urban areas for employment may be reversed as jobs will be available in the tourism industry;
- increase in youth exchange programmes, village tourism, home swap programmes and voluntary work overseas.

Dubai is a good example of a tourist destination where the development of tourism has had positive effects on the social and cultural life of the area. As you will see in the case study in Chapter 2 (pp. 40–9), considerable financial investment by both public and private sectors has led to improvements in the infrastructure and to job creation. Archaeological and heritage sites are preserved, and local traditions maintained. The hospitable culture of the Arab world and acceptance of others' lifestyles means that tourists are welcomed but do not threaten existing ways of life.

However, tourism may have **negative effects** on an area, such as:

- the infrastructure (roads, railways, health care provision) may not be able to cope with the greater numbers created by tourism;
- poor sanitation may lead to diseases for both tourists and local population;
- local population's activities and lifestyles may suffer intrusion from tourists leading to resentment towards tourists;
- the local population may copy lifestyles of tourists through the 'demonstration effect' and the result could be a loss to local customs and traditions as well as standards of behaviour;
- there could be a loss of native languages and traditions leading to the area losing some of its original appeal;
- increased crime could develop through a decline in moral and religious values, leading to greed and jealousy of wealthier visitors;

- traditional industries may be lost and local goods substituted by imported and mass-produced goods which lack authenticity but appeal to a mass market;
- tourists may act in an anti-social manner which could cause offence to the local population. Unless sufficient information is provided by the host nation and tourist providers on the standards of behaviour expected in that area, local populations may come to resent tourists and act aggressively towards them, or the host community adopts the same anti-social behaviour;
- tourists may be unprepared for social contact and interaction with the host community (particularly in large self-contained resort areas) which leads to resentment and constraint in the host community;
- there may be language barriers between the tourist and the host community which may create communication problems.

Providing careful planning is undertaken in an area where tourist development is being considered and the host community fully involved in that planning, many of these negative factors can be overcome. However, some of the negative factors may take some time to become apparent in the host community so planners need to research tourist development and its effects to try and prevent problems arising.

Economic impacts of tourism

The major benefit of tourism for a region or country is economic as it provides an opportunity for job creation and generation of revenue at international, national, regional and local levels. Tourism can also benefit economies at regional and local levels, as money comes into urban and rural areas which in turn stimulates new business enterprises and promotes a more positive image in an area. As an example, we could look at figures for the UK to show the level of spending on tourism in 2000:

Spending by visitors from overseas	£ billion
Visits to the UK	12.8
Fares to UK carriers	3.5
Spending by domestic tourists	
Trips of 1+ nights	26.1
Day trips	32.7

◀ Spending on tourism in 2000

In the UK tourism accounts for around 4 per cent of GDP (Gross Domestic Product) and employs 1.8 million people. (Gross Domestic Product is the total value of goods and services produced in the country plus its net revenues from abroad. Studying the contribution of tourism to a country's GDP can give an indication of the importance of tourism in relation to other industries in that country.) Globally, the World Travel and Tourism Council indicated that in 1996 tourism generated a total output of US$3.6 trillion and contributed 10.7 per cent of global Gross Domestic Product. Many governments now actively promote tourism in order to bring foreign currency into a country and generate more wealth for that country. The income generated helps the national balance of payments, earning revenue through direct taxation, as well as from indirect taxes on goods and services purchased by tourists.

When an area develops as a tourist destination, the local economy benefits because new jobs are created and visitors bring more business to local shops and restaurants. The income generated can then be used to improve local services, whether by developing better transport and infrastructure, or by providing more facilities for residents and visitors, such as leisure centres, shopping areas and entertainment or attractions. This is known as the '**multiplier effect**'.

Activity

Look at the pie chart below, showing the domestic and overseas tourist spending breakdown for the UK in 1999. Obtain similar statistics for your own area and compare the percentages in each of the principal areas.

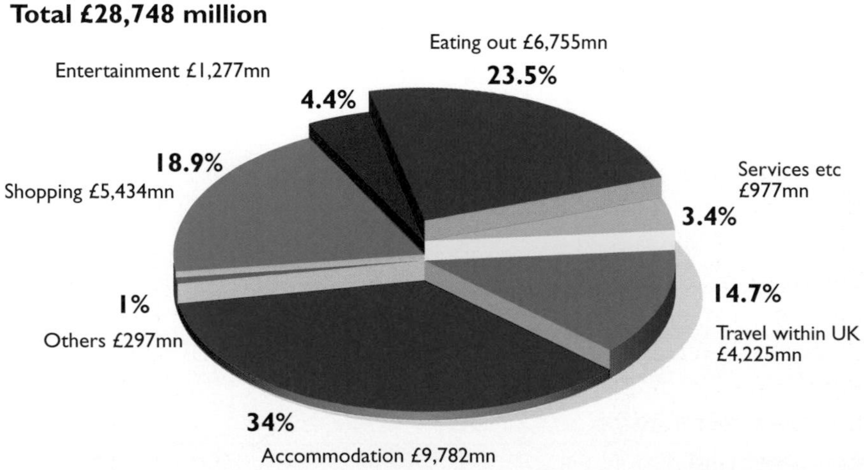

Total £28,748 million

Figure 5 ▶
UK tourist spending breakdown, 1999

Source: www.staruk.org.uk, sponsored by the National Tourist Boards and the Department for Culture, Media and Sport

The **balance of payments** is a statement which shows the flows of international currency and capital items to and from a particular country. Items are classed as either 'visible' or 'invisible'. Visibles are items which can be seen – such as cars, electrical products or raw materials – and invisible items are those which cannot be physically seen – such as shipping, banking, tourism and insurance. The tourism balance of payments for a particular country is the figure which shows all the earnings from overseas visitors, less any payments made by its own residents who travel abroad.

If we use the figures for the UK we can see how the tourism balance of payments has changed over a period of time:

	1975	1987	1996	1997	1998
Money spent in UK by overseas residents	1,218	6,260	12,290	12,244	12,671
Money spent abroad by UK residents	917	7,280	16,223	16,931	19,489
Balance on travel account	301	−1,202	−3,933	−4,687	−6,819

◄ Spending on tourism 1975–98, in £ millions

Source: National Statistics for the UK

Using these figures, it is evident that the tourism balance of payments for the UK is in deficit (i.e. more money is going out of the country than coming in) and obviously the BTA has the target to improve this balance and reduce the deficit. One of the problems for the UK is that most regional tourism tends to be seasonal. In other words it is affected by weather patterns, with the bulk of tourism occurring in the summer months, though London and other larger cities may attract visitors throughout the year. Other countries may also be affected by weather patterns, such as monsoon or hurricane seasons, or some may attract particular types of visitors in specific seasons, such as ski and winter sports resorts.

The **multiplier** concept is the term used to calculate the benefit of tourism income to a particular region. Money spent by tourists in a destination area has both direct and indirect economic benefits. Enterprises which offer tourist facilities, such as hotels, attractions and transport operators, benefit directly from tourist spending. Other businesses may also benefit from the presence of the tourist, such as shops, banks, and businesses which provide goods and services for the tourist (like laundries and food suppliers). If visitors to London, for example, stay overnight, they will have to pay the hotel for the accommodation. The hotel uses this income to pay its staff and suppliers. Those staff will spend some of their wages in local shops and the suppliers will pay their own staff. So the money is circulating in the area and thus creating more wealth in that area for other businesses. However, a portion of the visitor's payment to the hotel is lost to the area, through taxation paid by the hotel to the government, or to suppliers outside the local area. This is known as 'leakage' from the local economy.

A small local restaurant is more likely to have a higher income multiplier effect, as it would use local staff and probably local suppliers. But a large city-centre hotel may be part of a national or international chain, and goods and services may be purchased centrally by the organisation, so less of the income earned by the hotel is spent in the local area.

Tourism is a very people-oriented business, therefore the opportunity to create **employment** in an area is one of the attractions to governments. If an area has suffered from declining industries and levels of unemployment are high, tourism could be a way of revitalising that area and creating employment. But the skills needed within the industry may not be the same as the traditional industry, so efforts are made to retrain and recruit those with the necessary expertise (such as communication, personal presentation or specific catering qualifications, for example). Some of the employees may need to be relocated to the developing area, particularly where there are skills shortages, but others will be employed locally. Other local residents may see an opportunity to become self-employed and develop their own business in the tourism sector. An example of this may be the owner of a farm in a declining area converting buildings into holiday cottages, or a fisherman unable to earn sufficient income through fishing alone offering boating or fishing trips to visitors round the local coastline.

Direct employment in tourism occurs in accommodation and catering, transport operations, travel agencies, tour operators, tourist attractions and government departments (such as tourist boards and tourism information centres, national parks and monuments, air traffic control and lifeguards). Tourism employment opportunities may also arise more indirectly, through areas such as customs and immigration officials at land borders, ports and airports; and capital investment jobs (design and construction of highways, airports, aircraft, hotels/resorts and cruise ships, for example). Employment opportunities may also grow in areas concerned with the supply and production of travel products (film developers, sign makers, laundries, food producers and chemists, for example).

The **negative impact** of employment within the tourism industry can be that, as the work may be seasonal, the employees may not have the same loyalty and commitment to the job, and take little interest in gaining skills and qualifications in the industry. The hours can be long and the pay may not always compete favourably with other industries, so potential employees may not see their work as a career opportunity. This can have an effect on the way tourists experience an area. Poor service or an otherwise unfavourable experience may affect a tourist's enjoyment of an area. The tourist is unlikely to return to that area and may tell others, thus creating a decline in demand affecting other tourism providers in that area.

Tourism is considered to be a growth industry, but if potential visitors do not have the income to spend on tourism, a negative aspect could be a recession in tourism. If a developing country is **over-dependent** on tourism, then the economic and social problems caused by a recession in the industry could be great. Governments need to develop strategies to reduce over-reliance on tourism employment to minimise these effects. A further aspect of over-dependence is that employees may be attracted to employment in tourism-related work and leave their traditional primary industries, particularly in developing countries. This has the effect of loss of labour in those traditional industries, causing labour supply problems.

Another negative impact of tourism can be **inflation** in prices of goods and services in an area, which causes difficulties for the local residents. The businesses catering for the tourist may increase their prices to attract more revenue but the local population may not be able to pay these higher prices. Prices of houses in a popular tourist area may rise, so local people may no longer be able to afford to buy there. This can happen where houses are purchased as second homes or holiday villas meaning they are no longer available to local residents. A social difficulty could arise as younger people may be forced to move from the area in order to be able to purchase a property. Local shops and businesses may decide to cater more for the tourist market, thus reducing the facilities and choice for local inhabitants who may need to travel further for basic supplies of goods. If an area is spending money on the development of facilities for tourists, such as hotels or roads, then there is less money available for other capital projects such as schools and hospitals which an area may need.

Environmental impacts of tourism

An attractive environment appeals to tourists, whether natural or built, and the development of tourism in a locality will relate to the surrounding area. The term 'environment' refers to the physical setting in which tourism takes place – this could be coastal resorts, historic cities, mountain ranges, picturesque villages, sites of cultural interest including museums and national monuments – and which provides the stimulus for travel.

Tourism itself will affect the environment in both positive and negative ways. The following lists summarise these effects:

The positive effects may include:
- increased investment in the area (may improve facilities, access and enable development);
- conservation of features encouraged (buildings, wildlife, countryside);
- increased income for upkeep and preservation of facilities.

On the other hand, negative aspects could include:
- appealing environment spoilt by over-development;
- local people displaced due to development of coastal resorts;
- damage to natural flora and fauna;
- scarcity or reduction in water supply/quality to meet tourism demands;
- increased litter and waste disposal problems;
- greater air pollution and noise from overcrowded facilities/increased air traffic.

There are pressure groups who campaign to preserve the environment and try to prevent over-development, such as Friends of the Earth and Tourism Concern. Government departments in many countries aim to achieve sensitive tourism development that is respectful of local environments and customs. The more involved a local community is with the development of tourism in an area, the less damaging the impact of tourism may be on that area. However, the local community may see the benefits of tourism development without being fully aware of the negative effects or costs to the community. Or they may focus on the threats to the environment without seeing the positive aspects. This is where local tourism forums (such as regional tourist boards) can help focus the issues and provide an opportunity for discussion and analysis as well as raising public awareness.

Activity

Select a town or region in your own country where tourism is developing or being considered. Collect newspaper articles which may be for or against the development or undertake a survey within the community to establish:

- the economic impacts of the development to the community
- the social impacts
- the cultural impacts
- the environmental impacts.

Having gathered the data present an analysis of the findings and prepare a report on the feasibility of tourism development in that area.

Role of national governments in forming tourism policy and promotion

As discussed earlier in this chapter (see pp. 12–13), national governments can have a crucial role to play in the development of tourism in a country. A government may set up a specific 'quango' (quasi-autonomous non-governmental organisation) to develop tourism, or have a government department with a minister whose special responsibility is the development of tourism in that country. The main functions of a national tourism organisation were outlined on pp. 13–14 earlier. The chief executive reports to the relevant minister, or if a similar structure is repeated at regional level, the chief executive would report to the national tourism board on behalf of that region. Some local authorities may also have a similar role and then they would report to the local councils. But the functions of all are to:

- establish a tourism policy – setting out the policies and priorities for tourism development;
- promote the area as a tourist destination – undertaking market research, marketing planning, producing brochures and other promotional materials and taking part in travel trade activities (such as attendance at international or national travel trade fairs and promoting an area's facilities to tour operators);
- ensure the infrastructure is adequate – providing or finding the funding for development of roads, railway systems, airports and transport terminals which are identified as necessary for tourism development;

- maintain tourist attractions and facilities – such as museums, ancient monuments, national parks and forests, historic houses etc.;
- ensure the provision of tourist information services – the NTOs often co-ordinate the provision of tourism information services for visitors, though they could be staffed and housed by regional and local authorities;
- provide legislation and regulation – governments may pass laws or regulations which relate to the provision of tourism services in the areas of, for example, health and safety, consumer protection, registration of accommodation and attractions, passport and visa requirements and transport restrictions;
- offer finance for development – by the provision of grants, loans, tax concessions and tariff reductions, in order to attract tourism development nationally or in a particular region;
- provide advisory services and training – these may be provided to businesses in order to improve their standards of operation, such as customer care, management skills, business enterprise schemes, to develop a higher level of tourism provision and service.

Activity

Find out who has overall responsibility for the development of tourism in your country. Investigate how this is administered and funded at both national and regional level. You may decide to invite a member of your regional tourism board to your centre so that you can obtain the information and ask questions about any proposed future developments.

If you can visit the website of an overseas country, such as Japan, Spain or Singapore, you may be able to compare the approach and statistics from that country with your own.

Regional tourist boards may be partly funded from taxation through governments, but they may also have a more commercial focus, linking public and private sector organisations in order to promote tourism in a specific region. As was shown in Figure 4 (see p. 14), membership of a regional tourism board is very wide, including hoteliers, tourist attraction providers, local authorities or councils, guesthouse owners, educational establishments and even transport providers. Funding may come from additional sources, such as subscriptions from local authorities and commercial members, revenue from sales of advertising space in regional publications and letting space at regional travel trade fairs and exhibitions. As they focus on a specific region, regional tourist boards' knowledge of the needs, demand and provision in that area is great, and they can supply the national tourist board with detailed statistics. Regional tourist boards are able to respond to enquiries about their specific region, and they can have an important input into the planning and development of the area's infrastructure and facilities, to try and ensure sustainable tourism to the benefit of the local population.

The provision of **Tourist Information Centres (TICs)** within a region is also the responsibility of regional tourist boards, though they may delegate this function to local councils through their Directors of Tourism or Tourism Development Officers. These are often centrally placed in towns and cities and are a source of information to visitors and local people on the facilities, attractions, public transport and accommodation in the area. The role of TICs was discussed earlier in this chapter (see pp. 14–15), and is looked at in more detail in Chapters 6 and 7.

But not all tourist information centres are based within the home country. Some countries provide information for tourists at their own embassies or consulates in overseas countries. Potential visitors can contact them before they travel, using local rather than international telephone calls, to help them plan ahead and book accommodation and transport connections in advance. These offices also act as the base points for the issue of visas and other immigration information and act as representatives of the home country. As they have a direct link with the home country, the information provided should be up-to-date and relevant to the particular tourist's needs and may be more detailed than information provided through a travel agency or tour operator.

Obviously, with the expansion of internet services, it is possible for potential travellers to access information from websites around the world, and print out anything they need for future reference.

Patterns of demand for international travel and tourism

The 'World Tourism Organization' stated in 2000 that:

> tourism is the world's largest growth industry with no signs of slowing down in the 21st century. Receipts from international tourism have increased by an average of 9 per cent annually for the past 16 years to reach US$ 423 billion in 1996. During the same period, international arrivals rose by a yearly average of 4.6 per cent to reach 594 million in 1996.

Figure 6 ▶
International tourism
receipts (excluding
international transport,
in US$ billions)

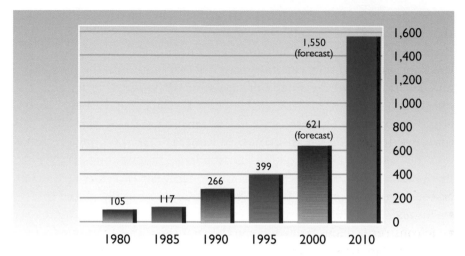

Source: World Tourism Organization

The World Tourism Organization forecasts that:

> international arrivals will top 700 million by the year 2000 and one
> billion by 2010. Likewise earnings are predicted to grow to US$ 621
> billion by the year 2000 and US$ 1,550 by 2010.

Source: World Tourism Organization's website – www.world-tourism.org

Figure 7 ▶
International tourist
arrivals

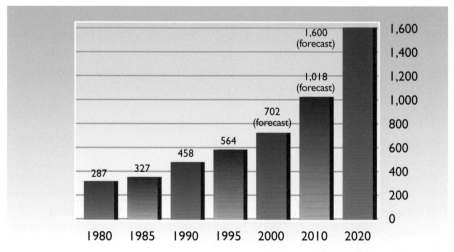

Source: World Tourism Organization

Both these charts reflect the increasing demand for tourism, which is the
reason so many countries wish to improve their tourism revenues from
internal and external visitors. One of the reasons for the growth has been
the change in working practices in some countries, with people having
more leisure time and more disposable income to spend on more than

the basic survival necessities. Another reason is that some countries have emerged from state control to develop a more 'western' economy. Examples are states which have become independent in the former USSR, or those whose governments now welcome the revenue from tourism, such as Vietnam, Cuba or Cambodia. However, where there is still some element of political instability, tourists may be more reluctant to travel. Examples of these could be Zimbabwe, Lebanon, Costa Rica and countries in the Middle East like Syria, Israel and Iran.

The WTO has offered help to many of these developing countries in practical projects such as:
- Tourism Master Plan in Ghana (1996)
- Reconstruction and Development Plan in Lebanon (1997)
- Action Plan for Sustainable Tourism Development in Uzbekistan (1997);

and in short-term projects targeted to address an immediate need such as:
- a pilot ecotourism development in Congo
- a hotel classification system in Ecuador
- resort marketing in China
- protection of historic sites in the Philippines.

Activities

- Using the figures you obtained from the Activity on p. 5 on inbound tourism and revenue earned from tourism for your country, compare the percentage changes in your country with the figures shown in Figures 6 and 7. Identify any similarities in trends and explain these in a short summative report.

- Undertake research in your country to investigate any involvement between your government and the WTO to influence the development of tourism. Or search the WTO website (www.world-tourism.org) to see if you can obtain details of the types of projects undertaken by the WTO in your geographical area.

The tourism industry has grown very rapidly since the 1950s, largely due to six basic factors:
- changing socio-economic circumstances due to higher incomes and increasing car ownership;
- developments in technology, such as improved jet aircraft and increasing use of information technology;

- the development of tourism products, such as resorts, package holidays, availability of long-haul destinations from national airports and the construction of all-weather attractions such as theme parks and sports facilities;
- changes in consumer needs, expectations and fashions brought about by increased exposure to mass media such as press and television, which has made people more aware of travel and tourism opportunities;
- raised awareness of health and fitness issues has led to increasing use of leisure and sports facilities and the development of such centres in hotels and resort complexes;
- interest in 'green' issues, such as conservation and preservation of flora and fauna.

As regards **trends** in tourism, the increase of long-haul flights has made more countries accessible to visitors from further away. The use of aircraft able to undertake very long flights has created the need for major hub airports to add to the number of runways and terminals and opened up tourism opportunities. Prior to the introduction of these long-haul flights, many places could only be reached by ships, whether liners or cargo ships. Even smaller islands now have their own airports with linking flights to major hub airports. An example of this is the Caribbean, where, though cruising is still a major tourist activity, islands such as Jamaica, St Lucia and Puerto Rico have developed larger airports to attract international flights and thus more international tourists, with connecting smaller planes to individual islands, such as Nevis, Mustique and Grenadines.

Another recent trend relates to changes in preferred styles of holidays. The traditional beach holiday is joined by more active water sports holidays. Tourists are moving away from the traditional package holiday into more individual tailor-made holidays. These might involve adventure pursuits, such as cycling, mountaineering or trekking, or they might be holidays catering for those who wish to be more independent (fly–drive, timeshare accommodation and short breaks, for example).

Economic factors influence the numbers of tourists visiting a particular country, as well as accessibility. Those countries where residents have higher disposable income (i.e. money to spend on luxuries after paying for the basic necessities) are likely to be the major **generators of tourism**. This will be explained further in Chapter 2 which follows. It is important therefore that the national tourism organisations undertake economic surveys in order to target their marketing not only to particular countries but to specific economic groups within those countries. It is also important that the NTOs are aware of the effects of extreme changes in disposable income of potential tourists. To use an example, the Japanese economic collapse in 1997–8 affected the disposable income of its people, who had to restrict their leisure and tourism spending, so affecting the tourist income of many countries popular with the Japanese visitors.

The figures shown below, for the UK, give some idea of the nationalities visiting the UK, and the type of income each contributes to the UK economy.

	Visits 1998 (000s)	Visits 1999 (000s)	Spending 1998 (£m)	Spending 1999 (£m)
USA	3,880	3,939	2,482	2,538
France	3,274	3,223	750	927
Germany	2,830	2,794	882	710
Irish Republic	2,310	2,075	824	594
Netherlands	1,718	1,617	407	560
Belgium	1,183	n.a.	225	n.a.
Italy	1.090	n.a.	555	n.a.
Spain	900	n.a.	396	n.a.
Sweden	676	n.a.	310	n.a.
Canada	673	n.a.	319	n.a.

◀ Visits to the UK in 1998 and 1999: numbers and spending

(Note: figures for 1999 only available for the first five countries)
Source: International Passenger Survey, Office for National Statistics

These figures show that the majority of visitors overall came from the European Union area, possibly because of its close proximity to the UK, and also because of trade links, as visitors include business as well as leisure travellers. It is interesting to note that in previous years Japan featured in this list, prior to the Japanese recession.

Also, it can be clearly seen that there has been an increase in the figures between 1998 and 1999 from the USA, reflecting a growth in the tourism market. According to the BTA, the UK ranks fifth in the international tourism earnings league behind the USA, Italy, France and Spain. When you compare the size of the USA with the size of the UK in area, then it confirms the fact that the actual size of the country is not relevant to the growth of tourism. What may affect the popularity of the country are other components of the industry or preferences of the tourist. Many of the visits could be for business purposes, but disregarding business travellers, what appeals to the tourist in these four countries – is it history, museums and galleries, climate or scenery? Unfortunately, the statistics have not been broken down sufficiently to establish the purpose of the leisure visits, and it is difficult to establish any single factor which makes one country more popular than another.

This section will be tested alongside the other three sections which make up the Core Module by an externally set and assessed examination. The activities which follow will provide practice for the type of activities involved in the examination.

Extension Activities

1 What do you understand by the term 'all-inclusive resort'?
2 Explain how large resorts create a variety of positive economic impacts, particularly when they are developed on tropical island destinations. Give examples of resorts you are familiar with.
3 Identify three methods a travel agent could use to make reservations.
4 Explain the social and cultural impacts that can result from rapid tourism development. Refer to examples you are familiar with.
5 Describe three roles of a National Tourist Board with overseas offices.
6 Explain briefly why large tour operators tend to have their own travel agencies and charter airlines.
7 Increasing visitor numbers can create environmental problems in many holiday destinations. With reference to a destination with which you are familiar, identify one environmental problem and explain how it may be solved.

Features of worldwide destinations

2

In this chapter you will look at the range of different places round the world that attract tourists. By the end of this chapter you will be able to:

- locate major oceans, seas, continents and cities
- understand different time zones and climates
- describe a range of different destinations
- describe features that attract certain tourists to particular destinations

This chapter covers Section B of the Core Module.

The main global features

Any study of the world's travel and tourism industries will at some stage involve the use of knowledge about where places are to be found. It is important that people who work in travel and tourism have a clear idea about the world's basic geography. There is much talk about 'globalisation' and it is quite clear that people are now travelling more widely and more frequently than ever before. To make sense of these recent trends and to appreciate their full significance, it is helpful to have a sound basic knowledge of the earth's main global features.

▼ Figure 8
The earth from space

Source: NASA

You will probably have seen this image before. It is one of the first satellite pictures ever taken of planet earth. The image is significant because it highlights the fact that the earth's surface is not uniform. It clearly shows that:

- the earth's crust contains both land (continents) and water (oceans and seas);
- the northern hemisphere has most land;
- the southern hemisphere has most of the water area;
- cloud coverage (i.e. weather conditions) is very variable.

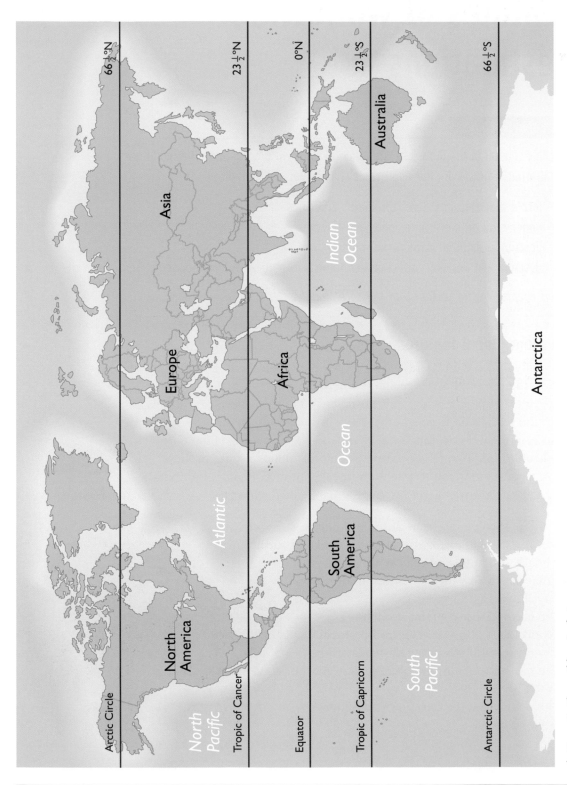

▲ Figure 9 The earth's major features

Arctic Circle

$66\frac{1}{2}$°N

North America

North Pacific

Atlantic

Tropic of Cancer

Europe

Asia

$23\frac{1}{2}$°N

Equator

Africa

0°N

South America

Ocean

Indian Ocean

Tropic of Capricorn

$23\frac{1}{2}$°S

Australia

South Pacific

Antarctic Circle

$66\frac{1}{2}$°S

Antarctica

You are probably very familiar with outlines of the continental and water areas on a map of the world, such as the one shown as Figure 9. Although naming these continents and oceans may not be easy for some people, a travel and tourism professional should have no difficulty in identifying the following:

- Asia (containing the Himalayan Mountains)
- Europe (containing the Alps)
- North America (containing the Rocky Mountains)
- South America (containing the Andes Mountains)
- Australasia (containing the Snowy Mountains)
- Africa (containing the Atlas Mountains)
- Antarctica
- Atlantic Ocean
- North Pacific Ocean
- South Pacific Ocean
- Indian Ocean.

You should make sure that you can accurately locate all the basic global features because there are other significant land and water features that it is important to know about. Some continents have famous mountain ranges that often attract tourists who are interested in activities like skiing, walking, climbing, photography and wildlife watching. The names of the important mountains in each continent have been placed in brackets in the list above.

There are also particular sea areas that generate a large number of travel and tourism visitors because of their importance as holiday destinations and/or travel routeways. It is therefore important that you are able to locate the position of the following sea areas:

- The English Channel (world's busiest sea lane, ferry routes)
- The North Sea (ferry routes, shipping lane)
- The Mediterranean Sea (beach resorts, cruise circuit, ferry routes)
- The Adriatic Sea (beach resorts, cruise circuit, ferry routes)
- The Red Sea (beach resorts, diving centre, cruise circuit, shipping lane)
- The Baltic Sea (ferry routes, cruise circuit, shipping lane)
- The Black Sea (beach resorts, cruise circuit, shipping lane)
- The Irish Sea (ferry routes, shipping lane)
- The Caribbean Sea (beach resorts, diving centre, cruise circuit).

Activity

Using an outline map of the globe, accurately name and locate these important physical features:

- the continents
- oceans
- main seas
- major mountain ranges.

Not all of the earth's major features are natural – man-made ones are probably of much greater significance. Travel and tourism involves the leaving of a particular location and travelling to a chosen destination. It is therefore very important that you are aware of the location of the world's **major cities** in relation to their importance as major **transport hubs and destinations**. Importance can be measured in a variety of ways but an examination of year 2000's air transport passenger statistics is very revealing.

▶ The world's busiest airports in 2000 (millions of passengers)

Atlanta (ATL)	80.2
Chicago (ORD)	72.1
Los Angeles (LAX)	68.5
London (LHR)	64.6
Dallas/Fort Worth (DFW)	60.7
Tokyo (HND)	56.4
Frankfurt (FRA)	49.4
Paris (CDG)	48.2
San Francisco (SFO)	41.2
Amsterdam (AMS)	39.6
Denver (DEN)	38.7
Las Vegas (LAS)	36.9
Seoul (SEL)	36.7
Minneapolis/St Paul (MSP)	36.7
Phoenix (PHX)	35.9
Detroit (DTW)	35.5
Houston (IAH)	35.2
Newark (EWR)	34.2
Miami (MIA)	33.6
New York (JFK)	32.8

Madrid (MAD)	32.8	
Hong Kong (HKG)	32.7	
London (LGW)	32.0	
Orlando (MCO)	30.8	
St Louis (STL)	30.5	
Bangkok (BKK)	29.6	
Toronto (YYZ)	28.8	
Singapore (SIN)	28.6	
Seattle/Tacoma (SEA)	28.4	
Boston (BOS)	27.4	

◄ The world's busiest airports in 2000 (contd)

Source: www.about.com

The figures show that over half of the world's top 30 airports are located within the USA. The USA is clearly the main generator of passenger air traffic and there are very few important locations outside of the main cities of the more economically developed nations. To illustrate this point more clearly, on a blank world map outline mark the location of the airports listed above. Some further points should now be clearer to you about the distribution of the world's major transport hubs:

- many locations act as gateways to their surrounding areas or hinterlands;
- not all locations are equally accessible;
- some locations generate far more traffic than others e.g. London;
- Africa and South America generate little traffic;
- Asia (the most densely populated continent) contains only 5 of the top 30 busiest airports.

We looked at the patterns of demand for international travel and tourism on pages 25–6 in Chapter 1. The fact that there are global variations should therefore come as no surprise. Some of the reasons that explain variation in levels of demand for travel and tourism products and services will now be investigated.

Time zones and climates

The surface of the earth is not uniform and we have already seen that there are differences in terms of the distribution of land and sea areas. There are also significant differences both between and within these areas. One such difference is to do with time, as there are a series of different time zones throughout the world. For example, if it is 10:00 hours in London it might be only 05:00 hours in New York.

Figure 10 ▶
World time zones

Source:
Oxford Designers and
Illustrators

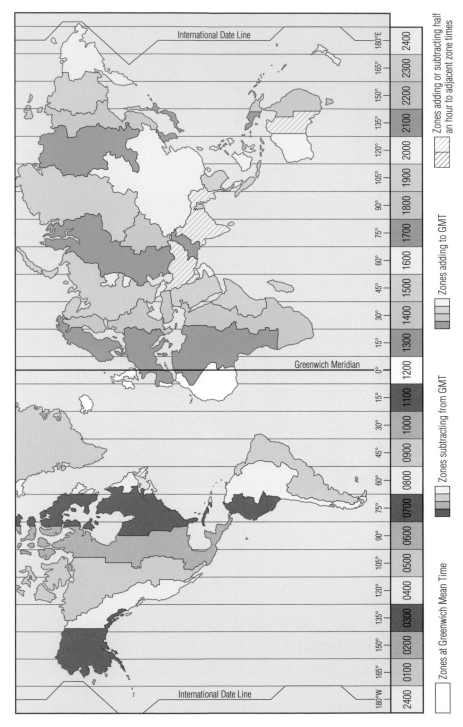

There is an imaginary line running from the North Pole to the South
Pole, known as the Greenwich Meridian. All time zones are set from this
line which runs through Greenwich in London. These various zones are

therefore always either a plus (+) or a minus (–) from Greenwich Mean Time (GMT). There are many published maps and sites on the internet showing the distribution of these time zones. As the map shown as Figure 10 shows, all countries to the east of Greenwich are a number of hours ahead and all countries to the west of Greenwich are a number of hours behind. Some large countries like Australia and the USA have more than one time zone running through them.

We all know that the earth is round and so there has to be a point where east meets west. Positions relative to Greenwich are indicated by lines of **longitude**, measured in degrees, from 0° to 180° East and from 0° to 180° West. The earth's time zones tend to correspond with particular lines of longitude, a pattern clearly visible on Figure 10. On the other side of the globe, directly opposite Greenwich, is positioned another imaginary line called the International Date Line. If passengers were to cross this line, for example on a journey from Los Angeles in the USA (behind GMT) to Sydney in Australia (ahead of GMT), they would go forward a day. Depending on the route followed and the locations involved, passengers might arrive at their destination on the day before their scheduled departure.

Travellers need to be aware of the additional complications that can arise when countries introduce Daylight Saving Time for certain months of the year. In the UK, for example, GMT is used during the winter months. This is then followed by British Summer Time, when clocks are set forward one hour, until October when time is changed back one hour to GMT.

The world map shown as Figure 9 indicates another change that takes place over the surface of the earth. The map has certain significant lines of latitude marked on it. You may remember from school geography lessons that lines of latitude indicate distance away from the equator, in both the northern and southern hemispheres. The position of any location on the earth's surface can be described in terms of its latitude, measured in degrees, north or south of the Equator. This is very similar to the lines of longitude, which indicate position east or west of Greenwich. The furthest point north is the North Pole (90°N) and the furthest point south is the South Pole (90°S). In each hemisphere, there are two additional important lines of latitude between the Pole and the Equator; these are the Tropic of Cancer (23.5°N), the Tropic of Capricorn (23.5°S), the Arctic Circle (66.5°N) and the Antarctic Circle (66.5°S).

The lines of latitude indicate divisions that allow us to make generalisations about the locational position of all points on the earth's surface. It is quite common to see reference being made to the following:

- **equatorial latitudes** (between 5° North and South of the Equator)
- **tropical latitudes** (anywhere between 23.5° North and South of the Equator)
- **sub-tropical latitudes** (between 23.5° and approximately 30° North and South of the Equator)
- **temperate latitudes** (between approximately 30° and 66.5° North and South of the Equator)
- **Arctic latitudes** (around 66.5° North and South of the Equator)
- **Polar latitudes** (anywhere between the Poles and 66.5° North and South).

If you have been able to plot the positions of the 30 busiest airports in 2000 on to a world map, it would now be possible to describe their locations using the above latitudinal descriptions. For example, in the northern hemisphere, the following illustrations might be offered:

- Singapore – equatorial
- Hong Kong – tropical
- Miami – sub-tropical
- Paris – temperate.

Arctic and Polar areas have no examples of major airports because of the harsh physical environments in these locations. The key factor influencing the climate of these latitudinal regions is distance from the Equator, and the influence this has on mean annual temperature. Most people readily understand that the Tropics tend to be hot and that the Poles are cold. Travellers to worldwide destinations frequently need to know what the **climatic conditions** will be like at the time of their journey. It is therefore very useful to understand a little bit more about the ways in which climates vary over the surface of the earth.

The characteristics of the world's major climatic environments can be summarised as follows:

- equatorial (e.g. Brazil's Amazon region) – hot, wet and humid all year
- tropical (e.g. African Savannah) – no cold season but summer rains
- tropical monsoon (e.g. India) – no cold season but heavy summer rains
- tropical desert (e.g. North African Sahara) – no cold season and negligible rain
- warm temperate (e.g. Mediterranean) – hot dry summer, cool wet winter
- cool temperate (e.g. USA/Canada border) – cold winter, hot summer, even rains
- Arctic (e.g. Scandinavia) – harsh cold winter with snow, cool summer with rain
- Polar (e.g. Greenland) – snow and ice prevail for most of year.

However, these are broad generalisations and there is considerable variation within individual categories. Visitors to foreign destinations will seek additional information from a variety of sources. Most holidaymakers will rely on information contained in their tour operator's brochure but independent or business travellers may well ask their travel consultant for information. There are a variety of publications used by the travel trade that contain basic climatic information about particular destinations.

Figure 11 ▼
Climate information for Bangkok (bottom left) and for Detroit (bottom right)

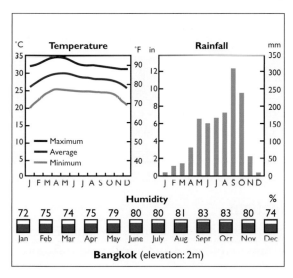

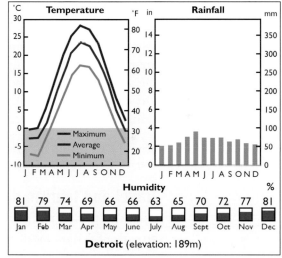

Source: *World Travel Guide 2000/2001*, Columbus Publishing

Figure 11 contains climate details for two of the top 30 airport destinations that have already been looked at. Information about the climates of Bangkok in Thailand and Detroit in the USA are given in graphical form. These types of climate graph are now commonplace and it is important that you are able to interpret them accurately. It is now more usual to quote temperature in degrees Celsius and precipitation in millimetres. You should be able to compare Bangkok and Detroit in terms of the following climatic variables:

- highest and lowest monthly mean temperatures
- annual range of temperature (difference between highest and lowest)
- wettest month and wettest season
- period of highest humidity.

Some sources of information will also list average hours of sunshine. They may also include the destination's height above sea level, because temperatures tend to decrease with increasing altitude. For example, although much of Kenya is equatorial, it occupies high plateau land and thus average temperatures are cooler, and it is significantly less humid, than in the adjacent equatorial lowland of Zaire. Such points will clearly be of interest to travellers contemplating an East African safari holiday.

Each major climatic zone may present natural hazards, depending on the time of year, for which visitors will have to make allowance. Travel consultants should be aware of the nature and location of these hazards. Some of the more significant ones for international travellers include:

- tropical storms (hurricanes, cyclones and typhoons)
- monsoon rains (see Bangkok's climate graph)
- monsoon winds (influencing beach conditions in Sri Lanka for example).

The climate of particular destinations is always a strong attraction for the visitor. The cold Alpine winter snowfalls are just as attractive to skiers as are the hot, dry and sunny December days around the Arabian Gulf to the winter sun enthusiast. The comparatively cold climates of north west Europe and north east USA go a long way towards explaining why their resident populations account for much of the world's holiday traffic.

We will now look in more detail at some tourist destinations.

Travel and tourism destinations

One way in which it is possible to examine the reasons behind the growth of certain locations as important travel and tourism destinations is to look at a particular case study.

CASE STUDY – *Dubai*

The rapid growth and expansion of Dubai as a tourist destination is a good illustration. Some of the statistics surrounding Dubai's recent developments are particularly impressive and few locations in the world can match the degree of economic diversification that the Emirate has achieved in a short space of time. In 1989 Dubai recorded only 630,000 visitor arrivals but numbers increased to over 3,000,000 in 2001. Dubai has managed to increase its number of visitors by 400 per cent in little over a decade and tourism is now, at 11.6 per cent of Gross Domestic Product, one of the most important and fastest growing sectors of the Emirate's economy.

Dubai's significance as a global destination stems from the fact that it can be viewed as an **amalgam**. It is not just a simple holiday destination, it is an important commercial, trading and business centre as well. Thus, visitors to Dubai provide

CASE STUDY – *Dubai* *continued*

examples of the three categories into which tourists are usually divided. The 1998 visitor survey in Dubai identified the following figures:

- 44 per cent leisure visitors
- 45 per cent business visitors
- 8 per cent visiting friends and relatives
- 3 per cent not classified.

Previously viewed in tourism terms as little more than a duty-free stopover, Dubai today has become a highly acclaimed destination offering an outstanding range of facilities and services for both leisure and business travellers. We will now look at some of the reasons behind Dubai's phenomenal growth.

◀ Figure 12
Dubai's location

Source: *Dubai 2000 Tourism Manual*, Government of Dubai Department of Tourism and Commerce Marketing

Figure 12 shows Dubai's geographical location (55°E, 25°N) on the southern shore of the Arabian Gulf. It is strategically located at the crossroads of three continents – Europe, Asia and Africa – a natural meeting place. Dubai is now a major aviation hub as the government's 'open skies' policy has resulted in Dubai International Airport being served by some 85 airlines, with connections to more than 130 cities worldwide. It is also the operational hub for Emirates, the United Arab Emirate's (UAE) national carrier. The UK is particularly well served with nearly 70 scheduled non-stop flights a week from Heathrow, Gatwick, Manchester and Birmingham. This high degree of accessibility, so important for the development of tourism, is clearly one factor in explaining the particularly high (550 per cent) increase in UK visitors to Dubai between 1989 and 2001.

CASE STUDY – *Dubai*   *continued*

Dubai is very accessible from a number of countries: London is seven hours away by air, Frankfurt is six, Hong Kong eight and Nairobi four. These facts give Dubai a very wide catchment area. Business events in Dubai attract delegates and trade visitors from around the world. This catchment area covers the Gulf States, other Arab countries like Iran, the Asian subcontinent, East Africa, Central Asia and the Commonwealth of Independent States (CIS – formerly the Union of Soviet Socialist Republics or USSR). This rapidly developing region boasts a population of around 1.3 billion people.

Dubai was also well placed to take advantage of the increasing global trend for leisure travel and to provide a different experience for an increasingly adventurous travelling public who constantly demand alternative destinations. The Emirate contained a mix of natural and cultural attractions that formed the basis of a very marketable leisure tourism product. The existing natural attractions included:

- miles of clean uncrowded beaches along the Arabian Gulf;
- sub-tropical climate with average temperatures of 18°C in January, 33°C in July and annual precipitation of less than 150 mm contributing to a year-long tourist season;
- year-round watersports in the Gulf (and the Gulf of Oman is a diving centre of international significance);
- desert dunes for a variety of outdoor activities;
- the Hatta Mountains for 'wadi-bashing' and other adventurous pursuits;
- the Al Maha environmental conservation reserve for the reintroduction of the Arabian oryx;
- bird life – Dubai is a migratory crossroads in both spring and autumn for many bird species (the Khor Dubai Wildlife Sanctuary is home to over 1,000 greater flamingoes).

Dubai also has a strong cultural heritage to exploit for tourism purposes. Important elements of this cultural attractiveness included:

- the 'exotic' Middle Eastern atmosphere associated with the hustle and bustle of the souks and dhow wharves along Dubai Creek;

CASE STUDY – *Dubai* *continued*

- the distinctly Middle Eastern architecture of the windtowers, mosques and palaces;
- its trading heritage, which means that the local population had a long exposure to, and familiarity with, foreign nationals' different ways and expectations;
- the traditional welcoming and hospitable culture of the Arab world;
- an acceptance of a cosmopolitan lifestyle.

These natural and cultural attributes have appealed to western visitors who are now arriving in Dubai in ever-increasing numbers. Although natural and cultural assets have clearly contributed to Dubai's success as a destination, it is very important to emphasise that they have been greatly enhanced by ambitious investment in the tourism infrastructure by both public and private sectors.

The Dubai Government's Department of Tourism and Commerce Marketing (DTCM) is the main organisation for the promotion and development of tourism in the Emirate. The Department has taken over the licensing of hotels, hotel apartments, tour operators, tourist transport companies and travel agents. It has a supervisory role covering all tourist, archaeological and heritage sites, tourism conferences and exhibitions, the operation of tourism information services and the licensing and organisation of tour guides. The Government provides ongoing development to the infrastructure and the recent opening of the Port Rashid cruise line terminal is just one of a series of innovations aimed at widening the total tourism product base within Dubai. It is hoped that this terminal will do for cruising what the opening of Dubai Duty Free did for air traffic arrivals.

The Government has a direct stake in the tourism sector through the development and ownership of a number of the major hotels as well as spectacular theme parks such as 'Wild Wadi'. This investment is not just a matter of expenditure, it is clearly demonstrating that quality must be paramount.

The recent creation of the 7-star luxury Burj Al Arab Hotel is yet another illustration of this underpinning philosophy in the

CASE STUDY – *Dubai*   *continued*

Emirate's development. Government commitment to the tourism industry is further indicated by the fact that His Highness Sheikh Mohammed bin Rashid Al Maktoum, Crown Prince of Dubai and UAE Minister of Defence, is not only the DTCM Chairman but he has been the driving force behind many of the Emirate's most spectacular development schemes. This level of government commitment to the tourism industry has helped to generate significant private sector investment. Hotel and apartment complexes have been extensively developed. There has been a rapid expansion in the number of local inbound tour operators offering a range of tourist experiences from desert safaris to dhow cruises. The result has been the creation of a world class tourism product for a world class destination. We can now look in more detail at the nature of Dubai's built attractions in an attempt to identify the ingredients of a successful destination.

A recent survey of UK tour operators promoting Dubai identified sport as being a significant component of the destination's appeal. The findings of this survey indicated that:
- 65 per cent offered golfing holidays;
- 10 per cent had packages based on watersports;
- 28.8 per cent had packages associated with Dubai Desert Classic (golf);
- 16.7 per cent had packages associated with the Dubai Rugby Sevens;
- 12.5 per cent had packages in March for the Dubai World Cup (horse racing).

The DTCM now actively promotes Dubai as *'The Classic Golf Destination'*. Dubai is home to the PGA Desert Classic and has several championship-standard grass courses that are open to visitors. Demand is so great that a central reservations office was created to manage bookings (www.dubaigolf.com). This is but one illustration of Dubai's well-deserved reputation for being the sporting capital of the Middle East. The calendar of events attracts top personalities from all over the world and a varied programme of different sports helps Dubai to function as an all-year destination. The variety of sports available is on a par with the best resorts in Europe and Asia, while there are others that are unique to the region. All the major hotels in

CASE STUDY – *Dubai* *continued*

Dubai boast very well-equipped sports centres and visitors will find floodlit all-weather tennis, squash and badminton courts, swimming pools, snooker, table-tennis and fully-equipped health and fitness centres at their disposal as part of their accommodation package.

Figure 13 shows features of central Dubai and it is possible to classify the built attractions in the following ways:
- shopping malls, like Wafi City
- traditional souks for gold and spices
- Dubai Museum and historical buildings
- business tourism facilities
- various luxury hotels in city centre or beach locations.

The concept of viewing a destination as an **amalgam** is very appropriate in Dubai's case. The important aspect to be aware of is that the destination combines different types of attraction with a range of other facilities in a planned and organised manner. The mixing of the leisure and business tourism environments within Dubai illustrates this principle particularly well. Dubai is well established as the leading exhibition centre in the Middle East and it was recently voted the world's best conference venue. The city combines the facilities and services of one of the world's major international business centres with all the attractions of a top destination. This means that organisers and delegates alike can count on effective and successful events staged in a luxurious environment offering an outstanding range of recreational opportunities.

The city now hosts more than 60 major exhibitions annually as well as numerous conferences, seminars, in-house corporate meetings etc. This demand is serviced by a range of business facilities including:
- Dubai Chamber of Commerce and Industry's conference venue
- major hotel venues
- Dubai World Trade Centre's 36,000 square metre exhibition hall
- Dubai Airport Exhibition Centre.

CASE STUDY – *Dubai*   *continued*

The business sector is supported by major local companies that are well equipped with a full destination management service covering hotel bookings, airport transfers, ground transport and a daily programme of tours and activities with multi-lingual guides. They also offer the required expertise for organising business-related travel, including original and exciting incentive programmes. The recent expansion of both

Figure 13 ▶
Map of Central Dubai

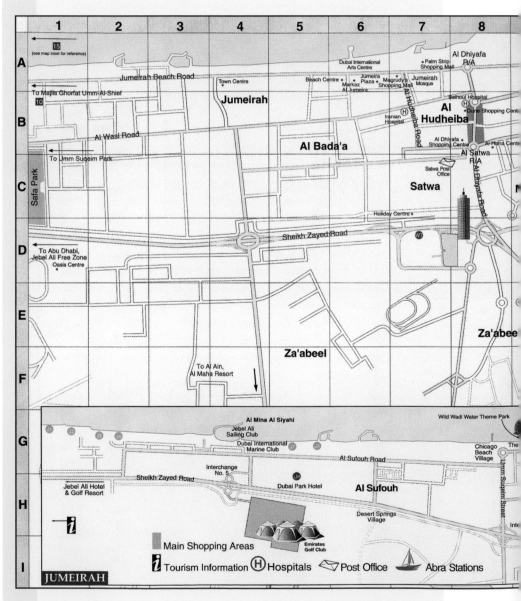

CASE STUDY – *Dubai* *continued*

leisure and business travel to Dubai has been matched by the growth in local inbound tour operations.

There is clear evidence to support the view that business and leisure tourism in Dubai have developed in parallel. Dubai's initial commercial development saw it rapidly become the leading port, trading centre and exhibition centre for the

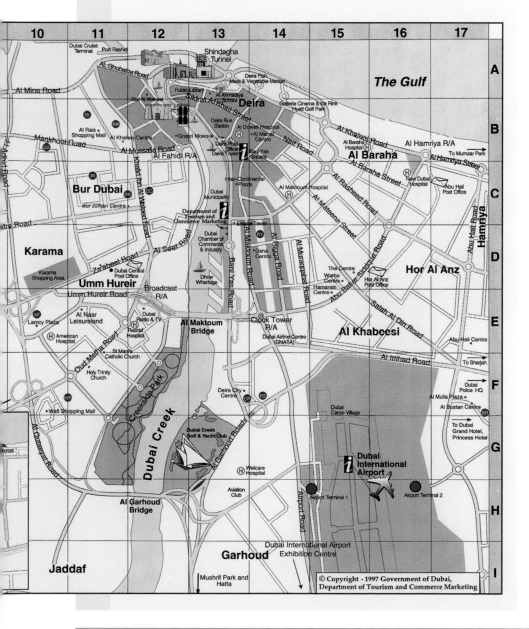

Source: *Dubai 2000 Tourism Manual*, Government of Dubai Department of Tourism and Commerce Marketing

CASE STUDY – *Dubai*   *continued*

whole Gulf region. The city thus had the basic tourism infrastructure of hotels and travel-related services from the early 1990s and these proved to be a very good starting point on which to build the leisure tourism product of the last decade. The DTCM markets Dubai as a destination for both leisure and business. The result has been impressive growth and the creation of development plans firmly to sustain tourism's economic impacts well into the future.

We can now end this case study of Dubai as a tourism destination by considering the attractiveness of one of the Emirate's premier resort hotels. Figure 14 is an example of the promotional materials produced by the Jebel Ali Hotel and Golf Resort. The property is set on a vast expanse of sandy beach some 45 minutes' drive away from the airport and city centre. The range of guest facilities is impressive and there has been a Dhs. 55 million (approximately 15 million US$) refurbishment to provide additional luxurious levels of comfort and relaxation for visiting guests. Apart from the features listed on the fact sheet, the hotel also offers:

- complimentary shuttle service to Dubai
- meet and greet transfers
- executive rooms on the Royal Peacock Floor and Royal Jasmine Court
- private business lounges and business centre facilities
- reading room, library and children's playground
- facilities for the disabled – with special room adaptations
- incentive programmes like the 'Club Al Safir' and 'Premiere Plus' membership schemes
- tropical gardens surrounding the accommodation blocks linked by a series of cascading water courses and a network of footpaths and bridges
- daily camel rides on the beach and a varied evening entertainment programme.

CASE STUDY – *Dubai* *continued*

Conference facilities fact sheet

فندق ومنتجع جبل علي للجولف
Jebel Ali Hotel & Golf Resort

Name:	Jebel Ali Hotel & Golf Resort
Address:	PO Box 9255, Dubai, United Arab Emirates
Telephone number:	+971 4 836 000
Facsimile number:	+971 4 835 543
Hotel classification:	☆☆☆☆☆
Accommodation:	389 luxurious air-conditioned rooms and suites, including 120 deluxe seaview rooms in low rise units situated in the Palm Tree Court.
In room facilities:	Safe deposit box, bathrobes, minibar, direct dial telephone, hair dryer and television with satellite channels.
Restaurants and bars:	8 Restaurants including French fine dining, Italian, Oriental, American Steakhouse, Delicatessen, Arabic and Seafood and 5 Bars.
Leisure facilities:	Catamarans, water skiing, windsurfing, gymnasium, tennis, squash, badminton, table tennis, horse riding, shooting club with pistol and clay shooting ranges, billiard room, deep sea fishing, four swimming pools including a sea water pool and children's pool, sauna, jacuzzi, massage, hair and beauty salon, shopping arcade, 9-hole Par 36 Golf Course, including floodlit driving range, putting green and pitching green as well as a golf academy.

Source: *Hotel Conference Guide*, Jebel Ali Hotel

CASE STUDY – *Dubai*   *continued*

The hotel was built in 1981 and has undergone a series of developments to bring it up to its present international standard. It is a member of *The Leading Hotels of the World* and has to meet the exacting quality control criteria for service and facility provision. The usual visitor services are provided for the convenience of guests and there are also special package arrangements to allow guests to visit the Hatta Fort Hotel.

Activity

To help you judge how well you have understood this case study of Dubai as a travel and tourism destination, use the material provided in this section to answer the following questions. These are the types of question that are frequently asked in the Standard Level Core Module Examination.

1 Identify three natural visitor attractions in Dubai.
2 Identify three built visitor attractions in Dubai.
3 Explain why Dubai may be said to have an accessible location.
4 Dubai has many facilities that encourage business tourism. Describe two services that help to support business tourism.
5 Define the term 'amalgam'. To what extent can Dubai be considered a tourist destination amalgam?

What attracts tourists to a particular destination

The Dubai case study has already indicated some of the ways in which a tourist destination can be attractive to potential visitors. However, there are many other locational characteristics that appeal to visitors and it is important that these are recognised. The appeal of a destination is only relative because visitor needs and requirements are so variable. Tour operators have progressively recognised this fact and it is now common to have particular destination packages aimed at particular visitor groups or market segments.

Information about destinations has been made available in a variety of forms. It is important that all international travel and tourism employees have the ability to extract relevant information from a variety of reference sources. This book cannot include examples of all possible

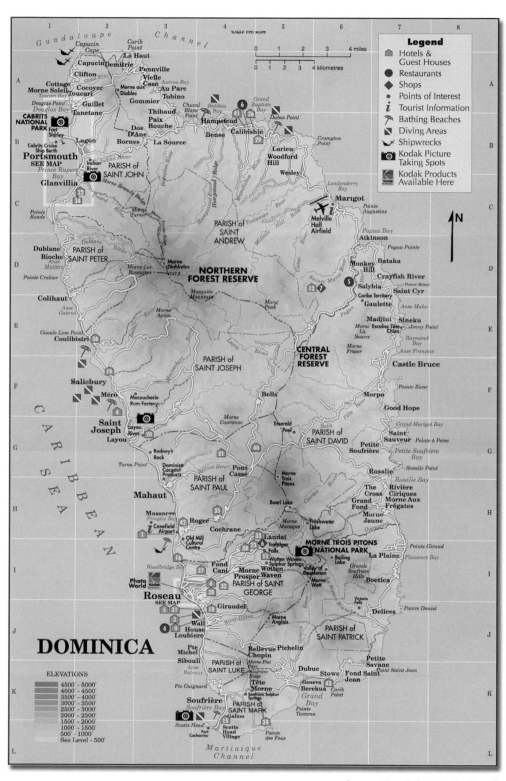

◄ Figure 15
Map of
Dominica

Source: Dominica Tourist Board

sources but attention has been given to those sources that are easily available and in everyday use. Figure 15 illustrates one such source of information. This is a tourist road map for the Caribbean island of Dominica. The map clearly contains information about the island's natural and built attractions.

Dominica is also a very good example to illustrate the ways in which physical features have influenced tourism development. The island is situated towards the northern end of the Lesser Antilles, lying between the two French islands of Guadeloupe to the north and Martinique to the south. The island is 29 miles long and 16 miles wide. It is volcanic in origin and ruggedly beautiful, with towering green mountains covered with dense tropical forests, deep valleys and countless streams providing magnificent scenic views. Dominica's physical features have created a unique selling point that help to set it apart from other Caribbean island destinations.

Dominica now markets itself as *'The nature island of the Caribbean'* and as *'The Caribbean's ultimate eco-destination'*. Visitors are attracted to the island to experience a range of natural wonders including:
- Morne Trois Pitons National Park – UNESCO Natural World Heritage Site;
- Valley of Desolation;
- The Boiling Lake – volcanic springs, second largest boiling lake in the world;
- Middleham Falls, Sari Sari Falls and Trafalgar Triple Waterfalls;
- 60 per cent of the island retains natural vegetation, the habitat for 172 bird species;
- 3,500 Carib Indians – descendants of the first native population – occupy their own territory and preserve the pre-colonial culture (Map area 6E);
- a wide variety of bays, coves and beaches with black volcanic sand;
- scuba diving, reef exploration and whale and dolphin watching.

However, the tourist map shown in Figure 15 also indicates how development of the island is limited by quite severe physical constraints. The 450-mile road network, although in well-maintained condition, provides only limited accessibility. Volcanic peaks, deeply cut river valleys and dense rainforest dominate the island's interior and such conditions make any large scale developments impractical. The island's steep relief does result in spectacular scenery such as steep volcanic sea cliffs around Soufrière and the Titou Gorge.

The fact that the island has not been extensively developed does make Dominica an excellent eco-tourism destination. The island's government recognises the importance of environmental protection and a series of measures have given emphasis to conservation principles:

- 1975 National Park established
- 1987 Cabrits Historical Park established
- spear fishing is prohibited
- removal of living sea organisms and artefacts from wrecks not allowed
- ecological resorts established, e.g. Papillote Wilderness Retreat.

The island has now become established as a Caribbean destination because of the quality of its managed physical environment. The strategy has clearly worked and visitor arrivals have increased from 47,000 to over 63,000 in recent years.

We have looked at both a tropical and a sub-tropical destination. We will now look briefly at some wider destinations in order to obtain a clearer picture of the ways in which differing customer needs and expectations can be met.

Cold climatic conditions and mountainous relief can combine to produce the ideal ingredients for the development of a ski resort. Winter sports holidays are now very popular and they attract a wide cross-section of visitor types. Ski resort development has taken place throughout Europe, North America and Australasia and there are now many established destinations for skiing enthusiasts to visit. One traditional destination is illustrated by Figure 16, an extract from a Club Med holiday brochure featuring the resort of Villars-sur-Ollon in Switzerland.

Two of the images contained in Figure 16 show traditional Alpine winter views. Villars-sur-Ollon is a traditional Swiss ski resort, set in the heart of the Vaudoise Alps some 60 km from Lausanne and Lake Leman in the Canton de Vaud. This sense of tradition will be an attraction for certain groups of skiers. The same traditional scenic appeal will attract summer visitors who enjoy exploring mountain and lake countryside. Winter skiers have over 100 km of pistes to try out within the wider Villars region with 45 ski lifts and 43 identified ski runs. The ski runs cover valley slopes ranging between 1,250 and 2,200 metres and this variation in altitude will mean that some skiing is possible early and late in the season, thus extending the resort's operational dates. The resort has access to 44 km of cross-country ski trails in addition to the downhill runs already mentioned. This choice of skiing widens the resort's potential appeal.

Figure 16 ▶
Details of
a ski resort
holiday

Villars-sur-Ollon

S W I T Z E R L A N D ψ ψ ψ

INFORMATION

ALTITUDE
1 300 m

LOCATION
Villars-sur-Ollon is a traditional Swiss ski resort of old, set in the heart of the Vaudoise Alps, 60 km from Lausanne, close to Lake Leman in the Canton de Vaud in Switzerland.

ACCOMMODATION
Our grand 'Palace' hotel is set at the heart of the resort. The hotel offers 219 rooms equipped with ensuite shower room/wc, hairdryer, telephone, television and personal safes.

RESTAURANTS & BARS
2 restaurants: varied buffets.
1 altitude restaurant at Bretaye. 3 bars*.

OTHER FACILITIES
Club Med boutique*, washing machine*, dryers*, photographer*.

CHILDREN
Petit Club Med* (2-3 years).
Mini Club Med (4-10 years).
Juniors' Club Med (11-13 years).
Children welcome from 4 months.

SPORTS
Full day ski school from Sunday to Friday: downhill skiing for all levels from 4 years, beginners' snowboarding from 12 years. Discover the mountains, guided walks with or without snow shoes from 12 years.
Snow garden: from 4 years.
Ski pass: valid all day, from Sunday to Friday. You must buy a lift pass extension* for the Diablerets Glacier.
Ski service* Club Med: 3 types of downhill skis for adults, children's and junior's skis, snowboards, snowblades, cross country skis, snowshoes and helmets for children.
In the resort*: curling, ice rink.

APRÈS-SKI
At Club Med: Americain billards*, video games*, karaoke, night bar*, Club Med evening entertainment.
In the resort*: swimming pool, aquapark, gym, squash, tennis, bowling, helicopter flights, cinemas, nightclubs.

Ski in style

Ski Domain: ski the domain of Villars which includes Gryon, Diableret-Meilleret-Iseran.
Between 1250 m and 2200 m altitude.
45 ski lifts.
10 snow cannons.
100 km of ski pistes:
• 3 black
• 27 red
• 13 blue
and 44 km of cross country trails.

Source: Club Med Winter Brochure 2001 (adapted)/Club Med Pictures

Part of the attraction of a skiing holiday is the opportunity to sample a variety of après-ski activities and Figure16 identifies what is available within the resort. The fact that this is a traditional ski resort means that the nightlife activities will be less extensive than in more fashionable areas. Older couples and families rather than younger singles and DINKY (dual income no kids yet) categories of guest may therefore dominate client groups. Indeed there is much evidence to suggest that the advertised package is aimed at families with younger children including the following:

- two of the five images feature children
- the package welcomes children from the age of 4 months
- there are three categories of children's club available
- the resort's ski school has sessions for children aged 4+
- there is a special 'snow garden' for children.

An added attraction for some people will be the fact that this is a Club Med holiday product which means that it is organised as an 'all-inclusive' package and therefore the hotel used will function in a similar way to all other Club Med properties.

To many people, the phrase 'Mediterranean holiday' will automatically suggest a beach holiday in Spain, France, Italy or one of the major islands. The Spanish Costas and the Balearic Islands have traditionally dominated Mediterranean tourism. The North African countries have a Mediterranean coastline and it is interesting to examine the ways in which they have decided to develop their own particular destination product. Tunisia is a good example to illustrate the roles of culture and history within the overall appeal of a destination. Travel consultants will often be asked for advice about destination products, services and attractions and one reference source available to them are National Tourist Board promotional guides. Figure 17 is an extract from the *Unique Tunisia* guide produced by the Tunisia National Tourist Office.

The extract goes into some detail about the many historic and cultural sites to be found within Tunisia. There is a clear marketing purpose in this as the country wishes to maximise its visitor appeal and to offer activities that will enrich a traditional beach holiday.

▶ Figure 17
Extract from
the Tunisia
National Tourist
Office's guide
to Tunisia

TUNISIA

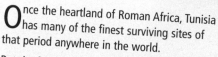

sites for sore eyes!

Once the heartland of Roman Africa, Tunisia has many of the finest surviving sites of that period anywhere in the world.

But the first visitors to the Barbary coast – named after the Berbers, the indigenous people of Tunisia – were the Phoenicians, who began establishing trading posts from 1200 BC. In 814 BC, Elissa (the sister of King Pygmalion of Tyre) arrived and founded a "New City" – Carthage.

Great prosperity followed and Carthage became a power to be reckoned with. As well as commercial ships, it had a war fleet of huge quinqueremes, propelled by five tiers of oars pulled by slaves, and an army of Berber horsemen.

However, Rome too was gaining influence and seeking naval dominance. This led to the hard-fought Punic Wars (246–146 BC). The first war was fought at sea, and ended with Carthage under Spanish rule. In the second war, the Punic general Hannibal led his famous elephants from Gaul (France) over the Alps to wage successful battles in Italy, but Rome's attack on Carthage itself brought him home to meet decisive defeat at Zama in 202 BC. The city of Carthage remained a thorn in Rome's side and the Senate determined: "Carthage must be destroyed." After a three-year siege (149–146 BC), all the buildings were razed to the ground.

The Romans then colonised Tunisia as far south as Gafsa, building magnificent towns such as Dougga, Sbeitla and Maktar all over the fertile Tell plateau.

Schisms in the church, the decline of Rome itself, and increasing attacks by the Berbers from the south weakened the country until its final conquest by the Vandals from Spain in AD 436. Little trace remains of their short rule. In AD 670, the Arabs arrived and, from their base at Mahdia, they spread their power across North Africa.

Today, the great sites of historic Tunisia include:

Tunis

The heart of Tunisia's capital is its 13th century Medina, a UNESCO-listed site that embraces a bustling marketplace amid a confusing maze of colourful, covered streets. At its centre is the revered Zitouna Mosque, where worshippers have been called to prayer for more than 1000 years.

The Bardo Museum contains giant marble statues, ancient ceramics and a breathtaking collection of Roman mosaics. On the outskirts of the city are the ancient ruins of Carthage, the setting for the legendary love affair between Dido (Elissa) and Aeneas.

The Dar Ben Abdullah in Tunis and Dar Annabi in Sidi Bou Said are excellent examples of traditional Tunisian houses.

Source: *Unique Tunisia*, Tunisia National Tourist Office, 2001 (adapted)

TUNISIA

Dougga

Tunisia's largest and most stunning archaeological site, Dougga, can be visited on day trips from Tunis. Most of its buildings and monuments are remarkably well-preserved, including a 2500-seat Roman theatre which is still used for open-air performances on warm, summer nights.

Bulla Regia

On the road to Tabarka, another compelling archaeological site featuring priceless mosaics left undisturbed for centuries. Among the ruins are underground villas once used in Roman times by the rich and powerful to escape the summer heat.

Chemtou

Chemtou was famous throughout the Classic world for its Numidian yellow marble, which was mined by slaves before being transported by river to Utica and then across the Mediterranean to Rome. The quarries remain, and a well-organised museum details the development of the site.

Thuburbo Majus

Close to Tunis, the elegant remains of this provincial Roman city include a second century forum, Capitol, summer baths and a temple to the god Mercury.

Maktar

Site of the Roman town of Mactaris, founded in the second century BC but rediscovered only in 1887. Among the ruins are the vestiges of a swimming pool, gymnasium and clubhouse.

Sbeitla

Site of the Roman town of Sufetula. The three massive temples dedicated to Jupiter, Minerva and Juno together provide one of the most memorable views in Tunisia.

Kairouan

More than 50 mosques are clustered within the Medina of Tunisia's most holy city, but pride of place goes to the ninth century, marble-paved courtyard and 400-pillar prayer room of the Great Mosque. The town is also a major centre for traditional crafts, including saddle-making and carpet weaving.

Monastir and Sousse

An eighth century Ribat with a tower overlooking the harbour is the major tourist attraction in Monastir. Historic landmarks in Sousse include the ninth century Great Mosque and a watchtower that provides an excellent view of the Medina.

Chenini

Close to the desert town of Tataouine, this 12th century Berber village perched on the edge of a mountain is famous for its unusual cave dwellings.

El Jem

Just over an hour's drive from Sousse, El Jem's third century amphitheatre – once used for dawn-to-dusk gladiatorial contests – is one of Tunisia's most spectacular sights. It is said to be better preserved than the Coliseum in Rome.

The extract indicates that Tunisia has much to offer those who are interested in antiquity and who have a sense of history. Attractions for such visitors may be classified as follows:

- preserved remains of four types of historical settlement: Punic, Roman, Byzantine and Islamic;
- remains of particular significance e.g. Carthage associated with the legend of Queen Dido, the post-Hannibal Roman destruction in 146 BC, the Arab invasion of AD 698;
- Kairouan, the fourth most holy city in the Islamic world, founded in AD 670 by a disciple of the Prophet Mohammed. It is estimated that the courtyard of the Great Mosque can hold 200,000 on holy days;
- some of the most important Roman remains outside Italy. For example, El Jem's Colosseum, which had seating for 30,000, and the Dougga Theatre built in AD 168 for 3,500, still in use for open-air summer performances in front of a 2,500 live audience;
- significant early Christian Church remains at Bulla Regia and Sbeitla.

The above examples indicate very clearly that Tunisian tourists may fall into a variety of categories. They may share a common interest in history and/or culture, but the precise reason for a visit to a particular destination may be varied. Some examples of this variation might include:

- archaeology students on a field trip would be an example of business tourism;
- Islamic pilgrims (according to legend, seven visits to Kairouan are the equivalent of one to Mecca) would be an example of leisure tourism;
- coach day trippers to Carthage on a resort excursion from Hammamet would be an example of leisure tourism.

Finally, to help clarify some of the more important features of worldwide destinations, one last case study will be looked at. We saw earlier in the chapter that Hong Kong is one of the world's most important destinations and that tourism contributes 5 per cent of local GDP (gross domestic product). We will now consider some of the reasons for this.

CASE STUDY – *Hong Kong*

Hong Kong is situated on the south eastern coast of China and is spread out over some 1,100 square kilometres, including more than 260 outlying islands. The main areas are shown on Figure 18 and include Hong Kong Island, Kowloon Peninsula and the New Territories. Hong Kong Island lies just south of Kowloon, separated by Victoria Harbour. Hong Kong increased visitor numbers throughout the 1990s reflecting its importance as both a leisure and business destination.

Visitor numbers are starting to rise following the decrease after the former British Colony was returned to Chinese control. Hong Kong is now being marketed as a city-break destination which is quite logical considering that it has been a popular stopover for long-haul Far East and Australasian passengers for some time. It is also an important cruise destination with over 60 lines using the Ocean Terminal. The appeal of Hong Kong is summed up by the Tourist Board's catchphrase, *'The City of Life'*.

We now need to consider some of the reasons why so many visitors are attracted to Hong Kong. There is a longstanding calendar of events that helps to stimulate visitor interest throughout the year. For example, tour operators featured the following special events when promoting their various packages during 2000:
- Chinese New Year (February 5–7)
- Spring Lantern Festival (February 19)
- Hong Kong Arts Festival (February 19–March 12)
- Hong Kong Rugby Sevens (March 24–6)
- Cheung Chau Bun Festival (May)
- Hungry Ghost Festival (August 12)
- Mid-Autumn Festival (September 12)
- Hong Kong International Races (December)
- Hong Kong Gourmet Delights – (throughout the year).

Besides these special events, there are a variety of standard tours that visitors to Hong Kong can undertake, which in their turn help to further enhance the destination's visitor appeal. The more readily available tours include:
- *The Land Between Tour* – to the New Territories past bird sanctuaries and country parks

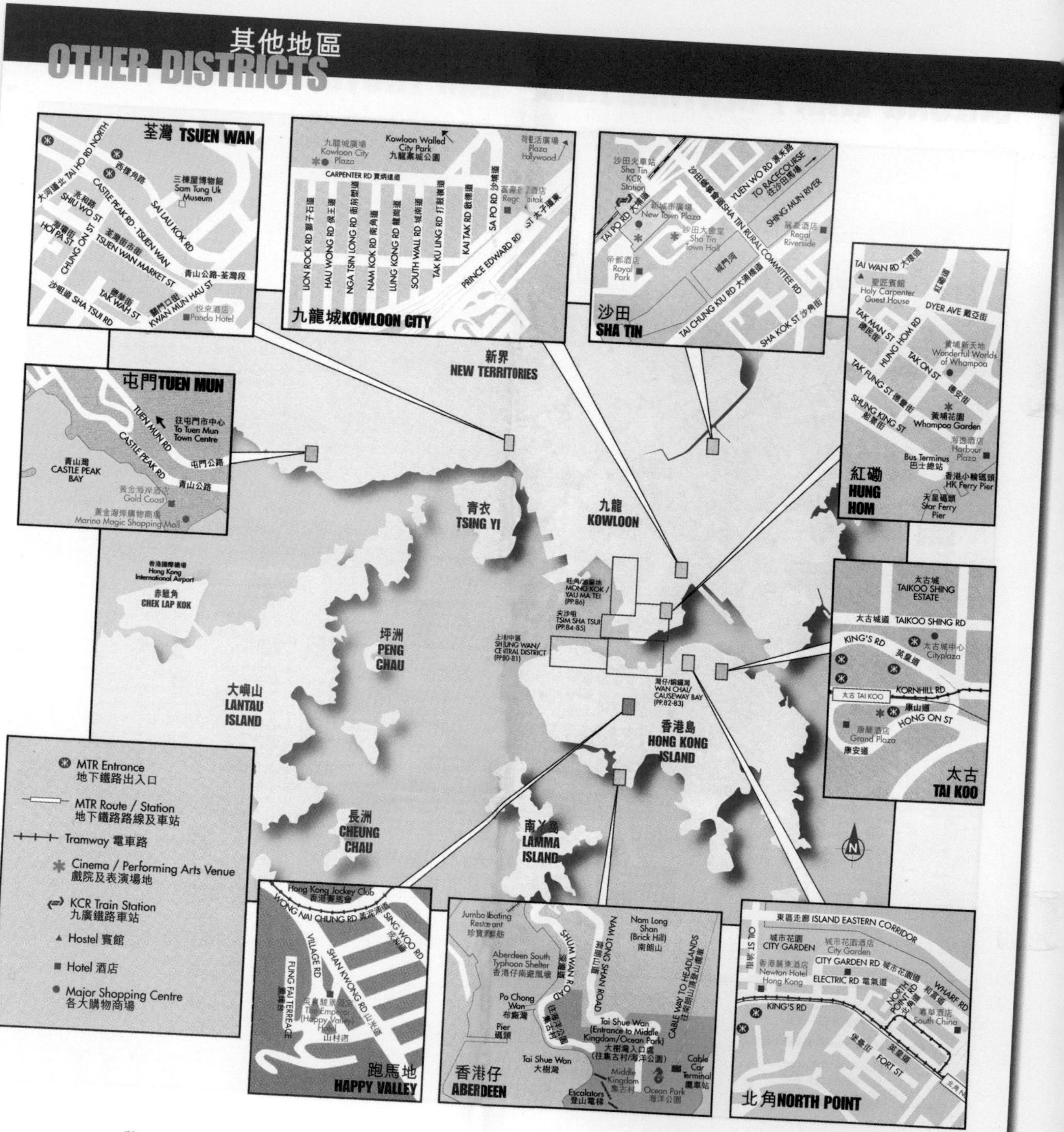

其他地區
OTHER DISTRICTS

其他地區
OTHER DISTRICTS

荃灣 TSUEN WAN

九龍城 KOWLOON CITY

沙田 SHA TIN

屯門 TUEN MUN

新界 NEW TERRITORIES

青衣 TSING YI

九龍 KOWLOON

香港國際機場 赤鱲角 Hong Kong International Airport CHEK LAP KOK

坪洲 PENG CHAU

大嶼山 LANTAU ISLAND

長洲 CHEUNG CHAU

南丫島 LAMMA ISLAND

香港島 HONG KONG ISLAND

紅磡 HUNG HOM

太古城 TAIKOO SHING ESTATE

太古 TAI KOO

跑馬地 HAPPY VALLEY

香港仔 ABERDEEN

北角 NORTH POINT

- ✳ MTR Entrance 地下鐵路出入口
- MTR Route / Station 地下鐵路路線及車站
- Tramway 電車路
- ✳ Cinema / Performing Arts Venue 戲院及表演場地
- KCR Train Station 九廣鐵路車站
- ▲ Hostel 賓館
- ■ Hotel 酒店
- ● Major Shopping Centre 各大購物商場

78

79

Figure 18 ▲
Map of Hong Kong

Source: *Traveller's Guide*, Hong Kong Tourism Board

CASE STUDY – *Hong Kong*   *continued*

- *Lantau Island Tour* – to see world's biggest Buddha at Po Lin Monastery
- *Heritage Tour* – historical sites such as a 2,000-year-old burial chamber
- *Walking Tours* – five walks enabling visitors to discover local culture and everyday life at their own pace
- *Hong Kong Island Tour* – views from Victoria Peak, Aberdeen and the boat dwellers and Stanley Market
- *Harbour Cruise* – around Victoria Harbour viewing famous landmarks.

There is a wide variety of other attractions that help to make Hong Kong a world class visitor destination with year-round tourist appeal. Hong Kong continues to offer some of the world's best hotels, fabulous shopping, spectacular views, Chinese and International cuisine. The city thrives on contrast; it is a modern urban centre with a strong and visible Chinese tradition and culture. It is a very appropriate location to begin any Asian adventure. The city remains a major international financial centre and many business travellers will have cause to visit the destination. Hong Kong's Convention and Exhibition Centre is in frequent use for major events and these activities attract large numbers of delegates and their associated staff. Many countries now have an ethnic Chinese community and there will be a steady stream of international arrivals who will be visiting friends and relatives.

Like many other important destinations, Hong Kong offers a range of recreational opportunities to both residents and visitors alike. There is a vast array of different types of nightlife, walking and hiking opportunities (40 per cent of Hong Kong is made up of country parks and green areas), 30 highly acclaimed beaches, and a wide selection of spectator sports. Clearly, Hong Kong enjoys wide appeal as a travel and tourism destination and it would be quite appropriate to view the city as an amalgam. There are many similarities with the Dubai case study.

Activity

Attempt an active comparison between one of these two destinations and any other one with which you are familiar, using the following headings:
- Locational details of global position
- Climate details – identify any high/low season
- Accessibility – major routes
- Natural attractions
- Built attractions
- Major events and cultural attractions
- Business facilities
- Visitor trends.

Use a variety of sources to gather the information and present your findings as a destination report.

To help you with your studies about the features of worldwide destinations, you can now attempt some additional questions about a completely different location. The questions are very similar to the types of question that appear in the Standard Level Core Module Examinations. You have to interpret the stimulus material supplied, and whatever is used will have been chosen to illustrate key aspects of travel and tourism destinations.

Extension Activities

Study Figure 19 on the next page, an extract from the 2001 *Liverpool and Merseyside Visitor Guide*, and answer the following questions.

1 Name three visitor attractions that have been developed in the Albert Dock.
2 Identify three hotels that are near the waterfront
3 Using only evidence from the map, explain why the Tourist Information Office near Williamson Square can be said to have an accessible location.
4 Suggest reasons why several streets in the central area have been turned into a pedestrianised zone.
5 To what extent can Liverpool be thought of as being a cultural destination?
6 With reference to examples with which you are familiar, explain the ways in which large city centre hotels provide products and services that meet the needs of both leisure and business guests.

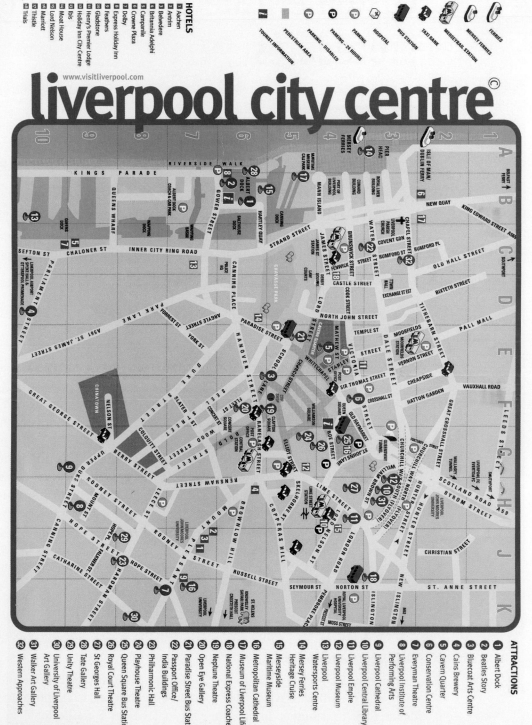

▲ Figure 19 Liverpool City Centre Map

Source: © 2001 Liverpool & Merseyside Visitor Guide

www.visitliverpool.com

liverpool city centre ©

ATTRACTIONS
1 Albert Dock
2 Beatles Story
3 Bluecoat Arts Centre
4 Cains Brewery
5 Cavern Quarter
6 Conservation Centre
7 Everyman Theatre
8 Liverpool Institute of Performing Arts
9 Liverpool Cathedral
10 Liverpool Central Library
11 Liverpool Empire
12 Liverpool Museum
13 Liverpool Watersports Centre
14 Mersey Ferries Heritage Cruise
15 Merseyside Maritime Museum
16 Metropolitan Cathedral
17 Museum of Liverpool Life
18 National Express Coaches
19 Neptune Theatre
20 Open Eye Gallery
21 Paradise Street Bus Station
22 Passport Office/ India Buildings
23 Philharmonic Hall
24 Playhouse Theatre
25 Queen Square Bus Station
26 Royal Court Theatre
27 St Georges Hall
28 Tate Gallery
29 Unity Theatre
30 University of Liverpool Art Gallery
31 Walker Art Gallery
32 Western Approaches

3 Customer care and working procedures

Learning outcomes

In this chapter you will look at the importance of customer care and at working procedures within the travel and tourism industry. By the end of this chapter, you should be able to:

- understand the importance of working well with customers and colleagues
- identify the essential personal skills needed in travel and tourism
- describe how to handle enquiries, make reservations and receive money
- identify and use a range of travel-related reference sources
- describe the presentation and promotion of tourist facilities

This chapter covers Section C of the Core Module.

All organisations within the travel and tourism industries are involved in the provision of products and services for their customers. Many staff within these organisations are required to deal with customers as part of their everyday work. Both commercial and non-commercial organisations share the same customer focus and aim to provide exactly the range of products and services that their customers want and need. At the heart of this process lies effective customer service. 'Caring for the customer' will lead to customer satisfaction and will encourage customers to continue using those organisations which successfully cater for their needs, as well as recommending the products and services to others. This chapter explores the real importance of travel and tourism organisations providing excellent customer care, and looks at ways in which this can be achieved through working practices.

Dealing with customers and colleagues

Customer care policies

A common feature of the induction programme for all newly appointed members of staff within travel or tourism organisations is guidance in dealing with customers. In fact, the vast majority of organisations, ranging from small independently run guesthouses to the vast multi-national tour operators, all have **customer care policies** in place.

A customer care policy is usually a written document which sets out guidelines about the most effective way of dealing with customers in a range of everyday situations. Staff working in the industry quickly find themselves made aware of the importance of putting the customer first. Part of their training will identify the reasons why customer care is so important to the organisation. These can usually be summarised under the following headings:

- Increasing the number of customers using the products and services of the organisation
- Creating sales income and generating profit (if appropriate, i.e. for commercial organisations)
- Encouraging repeat business
- Gaining a larger share of the market by attracting more customers than rival organisations
- Enhancing the image and reputation of the organisation
- Creating a workforce, which gains complete job satisfaction.

Increasing the customer base means attracting more customers to use the products and/or services of the organisation. It is important to retain existing customers too as both new and regular customers are equally important to the success and profitability of an organisation. New custom is often generated through the use of general marketing methods, whilst repeat business is created by gaining customer loyalty. Many travel and tourism organisations use promotional methods to retain existing customers, such as free currency exchange or travel insurance as part of a repeat booking deal. (See Chapter 5: 'Marketing and promotion' for more information about the techniques used by travel and tourism organisations.) Obviously the more customers an organisation has, the more likely it is to generate a sales income and, where applicable, profit.

All businesses require finance in order to stay in operation. Even organisations in the public and voluntary sectors of the travel and tourism industry have to make money, to remain in business providing products and services for their customers, despite being funded by government and other subsidised sources. The industry is dominated by private sector businesses, which must make profits in order to continue operating. The larger the number of customers, the more likely it is that sales income and profit generation will allow the organisation to remain in business.

Within an industry as large and as diverse as travel and tourism globally, there is a great element of competition between providers of similar products and/or services. It is therefore essential that each organisation aims to attract the greatest number of customers in establishing themselves within that particular market. Those organisations with the greatest share of the market have been successful in attracting custom away from their main business rivals and have achieved competitive advantage over these rivals.

The image and reputation of an organisation will greatly affect the way in which customers perceive the level of service they will expect. As customer care focuses on meeting customers' needs and expectations, this is a very important aspect of customer service. A satisfied customer tells on average two acquaintances of their experiences; a dissatisfied customer tells on average nine acquaintances. Word of mouth recommendations are especially important in promoting the product and services within the travel and tourism industry, so the power of company image and reputation is clear to see.

Staff who recognise the importance of their work and are rewarded for their achievements within the organisation are a powerful advertisement for that company. Frontline staff working within the travel and tourism industry who come into direct contact with customers are an important resource in promoting the image and reputation of the organisation. If staff have a high level of personal job satisfaction, customers will easily detect this. Equally true, those staff who are dissatisfied with their work will give a negative image of the organisation to customers.

It is very rare that a travel or tourism provider exists with only one employee. Even a small-scale, independent provider needs to employ several people to cover a range of job roles. Large-scale providers may comprise thousands of employees worldwide, each contributing to the travel or tourism product and/or service. It is therefore essential that each employee recognises the importance of their **role within a team** in contributing to the end product or service. As with any other business organisation, effective teamworking skills are required of staff in travel and tourism organisations.

Similar qualities and skills will be required of individual staff members in co-operating with other employees within different departments of the same organisation as are required in dealing with members of the general public. For this reason, many organisations will distinguish between **external and internal customers**. An **external customer** is one who has no connection with an organisation, beyond the use of its products and services. An **internal customer** is one who uses the products or services of one department of an organisation, whilst being employed elsewhere within the same company. The next section will examine in detail the wide range of personal and interpersonal skills that are required in dealing with all types of customers effectively within a travel and tourism industry setting.

Whilst it is every organisation's aim to achieve 100 per cent customer satisfaction, the likelihood of this is remote, especially in an industry such as travel and tourism, where customer expectations and the value of individual customer spend are high. Staff who work in frontline roles dealing with customers either face-to-face or via the telephone are therefore likely to be exposed to **customer complaints** from time to time.

Part of the organisation's customer care policy will set out guidelines on how to deal effectively with customer complaints as part of a quality assurance process. The aim of this is to pacify customers to such an extent that they feel their needs have now been met, whilst at the same time protecting the staff member from the abuse, aggression and similar types of behaviour that are often displayed by dissatisfied customers.

Most organisations will make their complaints procedure known to the customer in an attempt to provide a clear structure for expressing dissatisfaction. This goes part way to recognising that customer satisfaction is central to the success of the organisation and allows the customer to feel that their needs are important, even if they are not totally fulfilled from the outset. Similarly, most organisations provide comprehensive training for their staff in handling customer complaints, recognising the importance of maintaining a good company image and high reputation. The four most common reasons for complaints in the industry are:
- poor quality of service
- delays in receiving products and service
- being given incorrect information
- standards not meeting customer expectations.

Each of these types of complaint requires a different response and course of action. Staff need to understand how to react in any situation, and are trained to respond as effectively as possible in dealing with complaints to minimise the risk of customer dissatisfaction.

There is often a checklist detailing what steps to take in handling customer complaints as part of the customer care policy for an organisation. The following checklist provides an example of the sort of behaviour expected of employees in these situations.

Customer complaints:
Checklist for dealing with dissatisfied customers face-to-face or on the telephone

1 Listen carefully to everything the customer has to say – do not interrupt or argue.
2 Apologise in general terms for the inconvenience, to convey sympathy for the problem.
3 Inform the customer that the problem will be investigated and steps will be taken to put things right.
4 Remain calm and do not take the complaint personally. Even if the customer appears to be critical of you personally, remember that it is the organisation against which the complaint is really being made.
5 Find a solution to the problem and agree this with the customer. If this is not possible, refer the customer to a supervisor or manager, who will be able to deal with the matter.
6 Make sure that action is taken to ensure promises made to the customer are kept.
7 Record details of the complaint and what action was taken.

Different approaches are necessary when dealing with written complaints, although the general principles remain the same.

Activities

The Global Travel Company has received the following series of complaints from customers.

Complaint 1
'When I arrived at the travel agents, all the reps were busy. I queued for over 20 minutes before it was my turn to be served. Just as I approached the counter, another customer came through the door and reached the desk at the same time as I did, and was served immediately by the rep, who ignored my presence altogether.'

Complaint 2
'When I telephoned your office to explain the problems we had experienced at the hotel on our holiday, the rep who was dealing with my call was very abrupt. He said that I should write to the tour operator, as the hotel was not his responsibility, even though I had booked the whole package through your organisation.'

→ (contd)

Activities

Complaint 3

'I rang to check flight availability with one of your clerks, who said she would get back to me. After waiting three days, I telephoned again to be informed that the last seat had been booked the previous day.'

- If you were employed as Global Travel's Customer Service Manager, how would you respond to each of these complaints?
- What guidelines would you give to the staff who dealt with these customer complaints initially?

Essential personal skills required when working in travel and tourism

All staff who are involved in dealing with customers on a day-to-day basis will need to be equipped with the appropriate skills and experience of working with people. Obviously experience can only be gained over time, so it is important for new staff to have the opportunity of observing and learning from more experienced staff whilst at the same time trying to develop their own skills. **Personal and interpersonal skills** are not skills that can be taught at a one-off training event; they are gradually acquired by 'doing the job' yourself.

Personal and interpersonal skills include such things as:
- communication skills – verbal and non-verbal, including body language, gestures and posture
- listening skills
- telephone techniques
- dealing with difficult situations
- dealing with customers with special needs.

Many employers from travel and tourism organisations will specify the type of personal qualities that are necessary to succeed in effective customer service situations. These qualities may include characteristics such as:
- politeness
- patience
- calmness
- flexibility

- good organisational skills
- clarity of speech
- a smart appearance
- self-discipline, but an ability to work effectively within a team
- good levels of literacy and numeracy.

Some of these qualities can be developed through training and experience, but many of them relate closely to personality traits and the personal attributes of the employees themselves as they are innate qualities rather than learned behavioural responses. Successful travel and tourism customer service representatives often tend to be outgoing and friendly people, with cheerful and enthusiastic personalities, who focus more on solutions than on the problem itself.

Activity

Which of the common characteristics and skills given above would be most appropriate for staff employed in the following capacities and why are they important?

(a) Resort representative

(b) Air cabin crew

(c) Hotel receptionist

(d) Outbound tour handler

Different customer service skills are required in dealing with different types of customers. The next section will briefly examine how an employee in a front-line customer service position can quickly identify the nature of the customer before them, in order to select an appropriate response to their customer service needs.

Customer types are often classified under the following headings:

- individuals
- groups, families or parties
- people of different ages
- people from different cultures
- people with specific needs, e.g. restricted mobility or dietary requirements
- people speaking different languages.

Working one-to-one with a client allows travel and tourism employees to utilise their communication and listening skills most effectively. By using a range of open questions, it should take an experienced employee little time to identify the exact nature of the customer's needs and to decide how the organisation can best meet those needs. Dealing with individuals enables a good rapport to develop between the employee and the client, which is important in encouraging clients to feel valued and to encourage them to return for repeat business. This can only be the case if the employee is able to establish the appropriate form of contact with the client – it is as much about recognising the appropriate moment to intervene, as it is using the right communication skills in making that initial contact.

Listening skills are relatively easy to develop and demonstrate in a one-to-one situation, when compared with a group situation. An effective listener reflects back the statements being made by the client to check understanding and to demonstrate empathy for what is being said. This is far more difficult to achieve in a group situation, when several clients make contributions to a discussion simultaneously, to which the employee needs to respond in order to provide assurance that each individual's viewpoint has been heard and will receive appropriate action. Generally, working with groups of clients demands a greater level of expertise in communication than working with individual customers.

Examples of travel and tourism employees working with groups of clients could involve a small family booking a holiday together at a local travel agency, through to a school party checking into budget hotel accommodation abroad. Whilst it is usual for one person within a party to assume control of the situation, and to be involved in any discussions with customer service representatives, it is important to include all those in the group by making eye contact and using wider, more open gestures. If trying to address a large party to give information, for example as a resort representative at a 'Welcome Party', it is essential that the representative is able to throw his/her voice, so that everything is audible to the whole group. Each member of a larger party should be treated with equal levels of customer service; they are all customers, with similar expectations of their travel/tourism experience, whether or not they make direct contact with the providers at the facilities they use.

Communication techniques should also be varied to take into account the age of the clientele with whom you are dealing in a customer service situation. You would use a completely different tone of voice in dealing with a young child who approaches you for information about when the swimming pool opens, compared to the tone you would use with a more mature client asking a similar question. Older people generally prefer to be treated more formally, and appreciate employees who do not appear to be working under pressure and in a hurry. Children tend to need clear instructions and simple directions. Selecting an appropriate form of address and range of vocabulary matched to your client's age comes with experience.

Non-domestic tourists, by their very nature, are likely to be travelling to countries with different cultures from their own, and may well be non-native speakers within their chosen destination country. Their unfamiliarity with the language and culture could cause communication issues for travel and tourism employees. It is therefore important to consider the specific cultural and language needs of all clients with whom you deal and to discover the most effective way of meeting these needs.

Activity

Imagine that you are working in a hotel in a popular holiday resort. Design a poster for the staffroom noticeboard to encourage temporary summer staff to consider how their response to customers must be tailored to each individual client's needs.

Figure 20 ▶
Customer service representative dealing with clients

Source: Hotel Elizabeth Rockingham, Corby, UK

Personal appearance

Frontline staff at travel and tourist facilities are customers' first point of contact with the organisation. It has often been said that 'first impressions last', therefore the impression that customers first receive on entering an establishment is very important. The manner in which the member of staff first presents themselves to a customer can be the main criterion used by the customer in assessing the quality of customer service offered by the organisation. The quality of customer service can influence customer decisions about whether to use the organisation in future. Customers expect employees in travel and tourism organisations to be smartly dressed, of pleasant appearance and professional in the execution of their duties. Other expectations are associated with staff's attitude. An employee who is warm and welcoming without being intrusive and invasive would be the ideal for the majority of customers.

Tourists visiting an Information Centre, for example, have the expectation that staff there are knowledgeable about the area and the range of products, services and facilities that are available. They require staff to be able to understand their requests and to present details speaking clearly, with directions and key facts particularly well enunciated. Many like to have information relating to directions or prices written down for them to take away for future reference.

High levels of oral and written communication skills are expected of those working in travel and tourism. A certain level of numeracy is also required to help staff make accurate calculations of timings and distances involved and to work out costings.

Activities

- Prepare a checklist of the qualities and characteristics you would expect from the guide at a city museum.
- What different qualities and characteristics would you expect from a member of the baggage handling staff working at an international airport, if you were involved in a discussion with him?
- Why do you think your expectations as a customer might change, depending on the travel and tourism setting?

Staff working within the travel and tourism industry are amongst those in the forefront of using the most advanced **information communication technology (ICT)** available. The need for accurate and frequently updated booking information for flight and accommodation reservations has led to the development of sophisticated **computerised systems**. Customers have come to expect such technology to be available and for staff to possess an appropriate level of ICT literacy with which to meet these demands.

Other advanced communication systems commonly used by staff employed in the industry include complex telephone switchboard exchanges in hotels, telex, facsimile and electronic mailing using the Internet. Many companies have also developed websites, with online booking facilities, which also have to be managed by those employed by the organisation.

These developments in advanced technology demand that staff are both trained and experienced in the use of specialist hardware and software in order for them to make the most effective use of the applications available to them. This is especially important in being able to access reliable information in a short space of time when dealing with customer enquiries about accommodation and transport availability.

Source: Holiday Inn

Figure 21 ▲
Online availability
search and booking
form

Handling enquiries, making reservations and receiving money

Handling enquiries

Earlier in this chapter, we noted that identifying the precise nature of a customer's needs is the most important aspect of customer service provision. This is the main role played by customer service assistants who deal with telephone enquiries, face-to-face situations with customers, or who have responsibility for dealing with written or electronically transmitted information requests. Similarly, the guidelines set down by a customer care policy will assist staff in recognising the standard procedures they should follow in dealing with different types of enquiries. There should be quality assurance standards set in terms of how quickly written enquiries should be dealt with, and a response received back by the customer. Customer service assistants should have a good understanding of hierarchical structures within the organisation in which they work, so that they know who to pass unusual requests on to.

Customer requirements

These are normally categorised in terms of the types of needs customers have. For example, a customer visiting a Tourist Information Centre might actually have more than one need. Staff are expected to be able to make an accurate assessment of these needs in dealing with enquiries, but must remember not to make assumptions. For example, if a wheelchair user approaches a customer service desk, it must not be assumed that their request will be for physical assistance – they may simply wish to find out a price! The most common customer needs are for:

1 Information

This can be a simple request about opening times, prices or directions. Customers expect their questions to be answered quickly, confidently and accurately.

2 Advice

Customers will expect the information given to help them make decisions and choices about appropriate products and services that meet their needs. They expect staff working in travel and tourism organisations to have extensive product knowledge. Some will seek your advice in the decision-making process and will expect unbiased and balanced opinions to be presented, e.g. 'Which are the best restaurants serving vegetarian meals in a non-smoking environment?'

3 Assistance

Some customers may need practical assistance in using a travel or tourism product or service. This could involve a demonstration of how to use specialist equipment or a request for travellers' cheques to be encashed. Less mobile travellers may need physical assistance in, for example, boarding the plane.

Figure 22 ▶
**Wheelchair user
being assisted**

Source: by courtesy
of Wheelchair Travel,
Guildford

4   **A specified product or service and prompt and reliable service**
The most common customer complaints link to the non-availability of
products, and the poor quality of customer service. Staff working in
travel and tourism organisations should have sufficient product
knowledge, and be able to suggest a suitable alternative if products are
not currently available. The issue of poor service should be tackled
following the complaints procedures mentioned previously, to result in
a satisfactory conclusion for the customer, which restores the
organisation's reputation and leaves a favourable impression.

5   **Security and safety**
All customers will need to feel that their experiences of using travel
and tourism products and services are carried out in a safe and secure
environment. Hotel guests will expect to be able to leave personal
possessions in their room, without fear of theft; necessary health and
safety precautions are expected in the use of equipment and
machinery such as lifts, gym or leisure equipment.

Activities

- Identify the various stages an employee should go through when dealing with a telephone request for information.
- Compare these stages to those involved when dealing with a customer in person. Are there any major differences? If so, how do you explain these differences?
- List the steps that should be taken in responding to a written request for information. Use this to compare with the results from your previous two answers. What conclusions can you draw about the way in which customer enquiries should be handled?

Many job roles in travel and tourism organisations will involve staff in dealing with booking requests for the use of products and services at a time specified by the customer. In order to ensure customer satisfaction and to avoid confusion over which customers wish to use certain facilities at a designated time, it is necessary for staff to make an accurate **record of bookings and reservations.**

Every travel and tourism organisation has its own reservation procedure that meets the specific needs of its product and/or services to ensure that the customer's needs are fully met. Many organisations will use computerised systems to record reservation transactions. These reservation records are normally completed by a member of staff on behalf of the customer. However, with advances in information communication technology, it is becoming common practice for customers to be able to make their own reservations online, accessing organisations' database records, in order to check on price and availability of specified products and services. If computerised systems do not exist, employees will complete standard documentation manually. It is possible to produce a basic outline of key information required in order to complete a booking form, as well as to identify the next steps needed to complete the process.

Staff must ensure they obtain sufficient details from clients in order to be able to complete a basic enquiry form, such as Figure 23(a). A deposit or full payment is usually required to confirm the booking. Key information will include:

- Full name and contact details of the client – full postal address and daytime/evening telephone contact numbers
- Number in party
- Names of party members, with ages specified for children – discounts may apply

- Date required – arrival and departure date details
- Preferred choice of accommodation – e.g. hotel name, resort name;
- Price range sought – e.g. $ per person, per night
- Number and type of accommodation required – e.g. double/single rooms
- Special requirements – e.g. provision for children
- Meal arrangements – e.g. full board/half board/bed and breakfast/room only
- Linked services required – e.g. transfer arrangements to airport etc.
- Payment method.

Again staff must ensure they obtain sufficient details from clients in order to be able to complete a basic booking form (see Figure 23(b)). A deposit or full payment is normally required in order to confirm a booking. Key information will include:

- Full name and contact details of the client – full postal address and daytime/evening telephone contact numbers
- Number in party
- Names of party members, with ages specified for children – discounts may apply
- Point of departure
- Selected destination
- Preferred route
- Dates of travel
- Type of ticket required – First Class, Economy Class, Return, Single
- Cost of ticket
- Payment method.

GLOBAL TOURISM

CUSTOMER REQUIREMENTS & TRAVEL DETAILS

Customer Name		Home Tel. No.		Booked with G.T. before?		Y/N
Address		Work Tel. No.		Today's date		
		Ext.		Consultant's name		

TRAVEL DETAILS		ALTERNATIVE(S) e.g. if first choice not available	
Destination			
Departure Date			
Duration/Return date			
Departure Point			
Total of Party size	No. of Children Age(s): on return	No. of Infants Age(s): on return	No. of Adults
Accommodation			
Room Type/Meal basis			
Budget Range		Form of Payment	Booking today	Y/N

SPECIFIC NEEDS OF CUSTOMER? (*64# Short Haul *65# Long Haul)	Quiet	Lively	Beach	Kids Clubs
	Excursions	Nightlife	Activities	Special Occasion:

TYPE OF HOLIDAY REQUIRED–SPECIAL REQUESTS–FLIGHT DETAILS e.g. Class ....

CONFIRMATION OF ESSENTIAL & IMPORTANT DETAILS

Nationality of all Party Members	Passport(s) Held	Visa(s) Required	
Vaccinations/Health	Insurance Cover	Holiday Money	
Overnight Hotel	Car Parking	Car hire	

Call back ☎	(Y/N)	Reasons/Notes	
1. Date			
Time	(am/pm)		
2. Date			
Time	(am/pm)	Value: £	

Confirmed ☐   Provisional ☐   Enquiry ☐

▲ Figure 23(a) An initial enquiry form: Global Tourism customer requirements and travel details   Source: CIE

GLOBAL AIRWAYS BOOKING FORM
For reservations telephone 0870 241 0007

Please complete fully and return with remittance to Global Tourism (India), 3651 Ghandi Road, New Delhi.

NAME AND ADDRESS FOR CORRESPONDENCE

Mr/Mrs/Miss .... Initial .... Surname ....

Address .... Zip Code ....

....

Home Tel No .... Daytime Tel No ....

ALL OTHER PASSENGER NAMES AND DETAILS

Title	Initial	Surname	Insurance Delete as req'd	Date of Birth If under 18 or over 65 yrs
			YES/NO	
			YES/NO	
			YES/NO	
			YES/NO	

TOUR/OPTIONAL EXTENSIONS (Escorted Coach Tours, Rail Packages etc)

Tour Code	Name of Tour	Date	No of nights	No of rooms			Accommo Category
				Single	Twin	Dble	

SPECIAL REQUESTS/OTHER REQUIREMENTS

....

....

....

DEPOSIT AND HOLIDAY INSURANCE PAYMENT

A deposit is payable at the time of booking ($100 per person) or the full amount if within 8 weeks of departure.

Deposit .... passengers at .... = ...

Insurance .... Passengers at .... = ...

Full Payment .... passengers at .... = ...

Total amount included = ...

DECLARATION

Please reserve the holiday shown for the person/s listed above. I enclose a deposit of $100 per person or full payment (where travel is within 8 weeks). I also enclose the relevant insurance premium for each person traveling unless I have deleted the word 'Yes' from insurance panel on the booking form. I have read, understood and accept the Conditions of Booking and Insurance. I also accept that all persons listed are themselves responsible for seeing that immigration and health requirements are fulfilled.

Signed .... **Date** ....

METHOD OF PAYMENT

You may pay by cash, cheque (payable to Global Tourism), credit or debit card. If you wish to pay by credit or debit card complete the rest of this section.

I wish to pay by (circle card to be used):   Mastercard   Visa   Delta   Switch

Cardholder Name(please print) ....

Card Number .... Expiry Date ....

Signature of Card holder .... Date ....

Figure 23(b) ▶
Global Airways booking form

Source: CIE

Confirmation of booking

Once a reservation has been made, it is essential that clients receive written confirmation of their booking. This ensures that the details taken are correct and allows customers to make any necessary amendments. The booking confirmation also allows the travel and tourism providers to set out their conditions and to provide detailed information about cancellations, costs incurred and payment schedules. The confirmation will also provide information about further arrangements necessary to complete the whole transaction – i.e. when tickets will be issued, how balances can be paid, etc. Computer reservation systems are often designed to automatically generate confirmation details for clients. If computerised systems do not exist, employees will complete standard documentation manually.

Record of payment and the issue of receipts

Staff working in travel and tourism organisations dealing with customer reservations and bookings will also find themselves involved in the process of handling money. Payments will be made for products and services – in the form of a deposit at the time of booking, followed by a payment of the outstanding final balance, or full payment at the time of booking, depending on the circumstances. Staff must keep accurate records of monies received and monies still outstanding for auditing purposes and ensure that customers are clearly informed of the cost of their products and services.

Computerised reservation systems are often designed to automatically generate the payment schedule, allowing a record of payments made to be produced and to issue a receipt for any monies received. If computerised systems do not exist, employees will complete standard documentation manually.

Activity

Using a copy of the Global Airways Booking form (Figure 23(b)) or a booking form found in the back of tour operators' brochures, fill in the details for yourself to go on holiday to a destination of your choice. Ensure you understand which information to complete and write clearly to enable the booking request to be easily processed.

Using reference sources to obtain information

There is an enormous range of printed material already in existence which can help employees in the travel and tourism industry search for information about specific products and services. These sources are being constantly updated, extended and replaced, so it is important to recognise that the opportunities for research are limitless.

Employees in the industry must familiarise themselves with as many reference sources as possible, depending on what is available to them through the organisation in which they are employed. These may include directories and manuals containing timetable and tariff details for selected travel and transport providers. There may be a selection from the huge array of destination and accommodation brochures produced by various tour operators. Also local and regional publications such as 'What's on' guides for a specified area and season; national publications such as maps and leaflets provided by tourist boards and authorities; and other destination guides produced for this specific purpose.

Many organisations offering travel and tourism products and services have created **computerised information databases**, which can be accessed by staff working in tourism information services. **Central reservation systems** (CRS) can be accessed to check up-to-date and accurate information about airline fares and seat availability. There are many different 'gateway' systems now available that allow online enquiries and reservations, the most common being Sabre and Apollo in North America, Galileo and Amadeus in Europe. The Galileo CRS provides the most comprehensive data to travel agents, with direct links to more than 163 airline companies and other travel service providers. It also has facilities for Last Seat Availability (LSA) and Carrier Specific Display (CSD) to allow more detailed information retrieval by its users. Since the introduction of CRSs in the USA in the 1970s by the North American airline companies, technological advances have enabled fully integrated systems to be developed across the entire range of associated products and services – including exchange rates, excursions, car hire, travel insurance and hotel reservations. Many of the smaller accommodation providers who advertise online bookings are only able to do so because of the use of a system linked into Galileo or a similar CRS via the internet.

Gather as many different types of travel and tourism reference materials as you can giving information on accommodation, travel and tourist attractions. Try and obtain copies of local and national timetables for trains, coaches and airlines. Pick up leaflets, brochures, guides etc. from your nearest Tourist Information Centre. If possible, log onto the internet and research the online booking systems of any travel or tourism provider with which you are familiar. Ensure you understand what information is required to make a booking or advise clients.

Itineraries

An itinerary is a proposed plan of the route and destinations to be visited on a journey, giving details of dates and timings, methods of travel, and accommodation. Staff working for travel and tourism organisations are often involved in putting together tailor-made itineraries for clients, which meet the requirements of each individual customer. Figure 24 gives an example of an itinerary, of a tour in China, taken from a holiday brochure.

Use travel brochures and any other information sources you can obtain to plan an itinerary to meet the requirements of the following client:

Mr Levin from Germany is visiting New Zealand for two weeks in August.

He will be travelling with Emirates airline from Munich via Dubai and Singapore to Sydney, then with Qantas to Auckland.

He wishes to visit both North and South islands, to take in Auckland, Christchurch, Rotorua and Wellington.

He has requested that a motor-home be hired on the North Island for 5 nights.

The rest of the stay can be in hotel accommodation.

Cost is not an issue.

HIGHLIGHTS OF CHINA TOUR
10 NIGHTS TOUR

DAY 1 DEPART UK, fly from the UK to Beijing with Air China

DAY 2 BEIJING. On arrival in Beijing, transfer to the Marco Polo Hotel for 3 nights. Take an afternoon tour of Tiananmen Square, including Mao's Mausoleum. Welcome dinner in the evening.

DAY 3 BEIJING. Today's highlight is a visit to the Forbidden City, the former home of the Ming and Manchu emperors made famous in the film The Last Emperor. The imperial palace which was home to 24 emperors, dates from the 15th century and houses a huge collection of priceless relics from various dynasties. In the afternoon, we visit the Temple of Heaven, an excellent example of 15th century Chinese architecture. After dinner, spend the evening at the Peking Opera.

DAY 4 BEIJING. A visit to the Great Wall of China, 2,000 years old and the only man-made structure visible from space. After lunch, return via the famous Ming Tombs, including the Holy road.

DAY 5 BEIJING TO XIAN. A morning visit to the Summer Palace and lunch before your afternoon fight to Xian (formerly known as Chang'an). On arrival, guests are transferred to their hotel for a 2 night stay.

DAY 6 XIAN. Capital of the Shanxi province, this fascinating city is now one of the most popular tourist attractions in China. Visit the famous 3rd century tomb of Emperor Qin Shi Huangdi where 6,999 life-size Terracotta warriors and horses guard their master who was responsible for the unification of China in 2,000 BC. Discovered in 1924, the statues are fully armed with swords, spears and cross-bows and are lined up ready for battle. Other attractions include the Banpo Neolithic Village, the Wild Goose Pagoda and a Chinese Calligraphy demonstration at the Tang Dynasty Art Museum. Followed by the Tang Dynasty Show in the evening.

DAY 7 XIAN TO GUILIN. Spend the morning exploring the City Wall, the Chinese Muslim area and the Grand Mosque. An early afternoon flight to Guilin is followed by an optional tour of this city, including the Fubo Hill. Stay at the Guilin Plaza for 2 nights.

DAY 8 GUILIN. A full day to enjoy a cruise on the Lijan River, journeying through China's most stunning scenery, passing local villages on the riverbanks and the cormorant fishermen at work. A brief visit to the city of Yangshuo is included.

DAY 9 GUILIN TO SHANGHAI. After a morning visit to the Reed Flute Cave, we fly to Shanghai for a 2 night stay at the Regal East Asia Hotel. In the afternoon, there is a brief tour of the Bund area and a ride to Pudong to see the newly developed financial area east of Shanghai.

DAY 10 SHANGHAI. A morning visit to the Yuyuan Garden, Tea House and Jade Buddha Temple. Also, partake of a tour of the former foreign concessions and settlements in Old Shanghai. Dinner is followed by a dazzling display of Chinese Acrobats.

DAY 11 SHANGHAI TO BEIJING. A visit to the Chinese neighbourhood is on the agenda this morning before you fly back to Beijing and the Shangri-La Traders hotel in the evening. The farewell dinner features local speciality, Beijing Duck.

DAY 12 BEIJING. The morning is free for a final shopping spree. Depart around noon for your flight home.

Figure 24 ▲   Itinerary: Highlights of China Tour   Source: Sovereign Worldwide brochure 2002 (adapted)

Country	Buy	Sell
Australia	2.7028	2.889
Austria	€1.5734	€1.7174
Belgium	€1.5734	€1.7174
Canada	2.2396	2.4441
Cyprus	0.9183	0.9823
Denmark	€1.5734	€1.7174
Finland	€1.5734	€1.7174
France	€1.5734	€1.7174
Germany	€1.5734	€1.7174
Greece	€1.5734	€1.7174
Hong Kong	10.7371	11.9971
Irish Republic	€1.5734	€1.7174
Italy	€1.5734	€1.7174
Japan	185.78	203.84
Malta	0.6352	0.6901
Netherlands	€1.5734	€1.7174
New Zealand	3.2691	3.5391
Norway	12.4011	13.4011
Portugal	€1.5734	€1.7174
Saudi	5.2243	5.8643
Singapore	2.5376	2.8376
South Africa	15.9712	17.1212
Spain	€1.5734	€1.7174
Sweden	14.6091	15.9791
Switzerland	2.3044	2.523
USA	1.3906	1.5358

Source: www.rate.co.uk/exchangerates.html

◀ Figure 25
An example of a list
of exchange rates
for the UK

When making travel and tourism arrangements for non-domestic tourists, staff working within the industry will need to be familiar with **currency exchange rates** for popular tourist destinations. Customers may require assistance in converting quoted prices into their own currency and to check the most up-to-date exchange rates available. Employees must therefore have access to such information, and should be confident in making calculations and conversions.

Activity

Using the exchange rates quoted in the UK Exchange Rate table in Figure 25:

- Calculate the cost of a holiday costing Singapore $3,500 in £ Sterling.
- What rate of exchange is given on the purchase of currency in Hong Kong dollars?
- Convert £100 firstly into American dollars, then into South African Rand. What is the final amount – excluding commission?

Obtain up-to-date exchange rates from your national bank and make similar calculations between currencies of different countries.

Presentation and promotion of tourist facilities

This section will provide a brief overview of the **promotional techniques** used by travel and tourism organisations to market their products and services. A fuller explanation of these techniques can be found in Chapter 5: 'Marketing and promotion'. The importance of personal appearance and a professional approach was mentioned earlier, relating to the people who work in customer service with travellers and tourists. It is equally true that customers hold the same high expectations in respect of the working environment. In order to create a positive impression, the majority of travel and tourism providers have recognised the importance of creating a professional image through the presentation and promotion of the organisation and its products and services.

This covers the spectrum of promotional activities involved. If the organisation has an office or retail outlet which customers can visit, then visual displays are of great importance. The advertisements, leaflets and brochures the company issues must take into consideration all the factors associated with successful marketing. Website design is of utmost importance in this technological age, as customers can form an impression of an organisation by visiting a website from the comfort of their own home. Chapters 5 and 6 will look at these issues in more detail.

This section will be tested alongside the other three sections which make up the Core Module for the qualification by an externally set and assessed examination. The activities which follow will provide practice for the type of activities involved in the examination.

Extension Activities

1 The following is a list of ideal practice in meeting customer service expectations at a restaurant.
   - Advanced bookings taken
   - Friendly greeting given on arrival
   - Honest advice offered about the menu
   - Drinks brought quickly
   - Orders taken efficiently
   - Service unobtrusively but efficiently provided
   - High quality food served
   - Cleanliness of utensils, environment maintained
   - Accurate, itemised bill presented promptly upon request
   - Assistance provided with coats and belongings
   - Opportunity given to comment on standard of service.

Draw up a similar list of customer service expectations for guests at an all-inclusive holiday resort.

2 You are employed by your local Tourist Information Centre and a visitor asks you for information about what there is to see and do in the area, for a family with young children. Which information sources might you use, beyond your own knowledge of the area, to help you suggest suitable activities for the family for a 7-day stay in the locality?

3 If a customer telephones to complain that she has not received written confirmation of her flight reservation despite having paid a deposit, how would you respond?

4 List the three most important personal qualities you expect from a resort representative. Give reasons for your answer.

5 Which information sources could customers with special travel needs access during out-of-hour periods when planning a trip?

6 What are the benefits to the employee of an enhanced reputation for the organisation in which they work?

7 Name four essential details that must be obtained prior to making a hotel reservation from a customer.

8 What specific product knowledge could a customer at an airport check-in desk expect from the member of staff serving him or her?

Travel and tourism products and services

In this chapter you will look at the range of different products and services in the travel and tourism industry. By the end of this chapter you should be able to:

- identify and describe tourism products and ancillary services
- explain the roles of tour operators and travel agents
- describe the support facilities required for successful travel and tourism operations
- demonstrate the features of worldwide transport in relation to major international routes

This chapter covers Section D of the Core Module.

Tourism products and ancillary services

If products can be described as 'tangible' and 'intangible', then tourism products and services are usually 'intangible'. To explain this more clearly, if you buy sports equipment, such as a tennis racket, you can touch it and call it yours if you pay for it; this is **'tangible'** – holdable. However, when you buy a package holiday you cannot physically hold it, so this is referred to as **'intangible'**.

The products may also be **inseparable** in that all the components form part of the whole product. For example, when you buy a package holiday, included in that product is the flight, accommodation, transfers and excursions. Each component forms part of the whole product purchased and cannot be separated. However, if you are buying an air ticket only, this product can be **separable** as it does not form part of a bigger 'package'.

'Homogeneous' when referring to tourism products and services means that the product consistency is the same, no matter what the circumstances. This could only occur in the case of tangible products, such as the tennis racket. But most tourism products are **'heterogeneous'** because influences such as weather, attitude of staff, time of year and quality of food can alter the same product purchased at different times or by different customers.

Also a tangible product, such as the tennis racket, can be **stored** but many tourist products are **incapable of being stored.** For example if an airline seat is not sold it cannot be stockpiled and resold at a later date. If the holiday or airline seat is not sold by the departure date, this could represent a loss to the tour operator or airline, so in order to try and stimulate sales of available seats nearer to departure date, the companies concerned will undertake price reduction and discounting techniques.

Very few tourism products can be separated from the ancillary services. If a person buys a product, such as a yearly membership to a health and fitness club, they will expect to receive services. These could be free or reduced rate classes, access to qualified instructors, refreshments, shower facilities and ancillary products such as sauna and optional beauty treatments. It is difficult to separate the product from the additional services provided. This section will aim to identify some of the products and services as they relate to the various sectors of the travel and tourism industry. They should, however, be sufficient to enable you to differentiate between products and services, and between tangible and intangible.

The key terms in bold on pages 88 and 89 are part of the knowledge and skills criteria for the Optional Module on Marketing and Promotion (Chapter 5 in this book). They are included here to help you understand the nature of tourism products and services. If you decide to do the Marketing and Promotion Module, you will look at products and services in more detail. For this Module it is important to understand the types of products and services which form the basis of the tourism industry as listed below:

▼ Products and services in the tourism industry

AREA OF INDUSTRY	PRODUCTS	SERVICES
Travel and transport	Airline, coach or rail tickets Ferry ticket Taxi	Pilot, driver, cabin crew Catering availability Toilet facilities Entertainment (such as in-flight videos, music etc.) Terminal services and assistance (booking-in, mobility, catering, baggage handling etc.) Currency exchange Marketing and PR

→ (contd)

AREA OF INDUSTRY	PRODUCTS	SERVICES
Catering and Accommodation	Prepared meals and drinks Room with bed and possibly other facilities	Assistance of waitresses Kitchen staff to prepare food Cleaning and maintenance Supply of clean linen and towels Provision of ancillary services such as cots, high chairs Business facilities such as fax, photocopying, conference areas Currency exchange in large hotel groups Payment by cheque or debit card Marketing and PR
Attractions	Museums Galleries Theme parks Theatres and musicals	Guiding services Catering and refreshments Information sheets and programmes Toilet facilities Performers, musicians, support staff Shops at facility Access to currency or payment by cheque/debit card Marketing and PR
Leisure and recreation	Sports fixtures Health and fitness clubs Outdoor Activity centres and providers Camp sites Sporting goods retailers	Provision of equipment Qualified instruction Catering and refreshments Toilet facilities Advice and guidance on goods sold/products provided Marketing and PR
Business facilities	Conference and meeting rooms Fax, modem, photocopying machines Business lounge at airports	Secretarial support Catering and refreshments Toilet facilities Conference organiser support Tables, seating etc. plus OHP, flip-charts, etc. Newspapers, periodicals Access to power links for modem, fax, telephone etc. Currency exchange and varying payment methods Marketing and PR

From the brief summary above, it is easy to see how the various components inter-link and inter-relate. No one component works independently of another; though the tourist may 'buy' one product, such as a travel component, other aspects of the industry are also involved or available to support that component.

If we extend this to look at the role of travel agencies within the provision of products and services, the inter-relationship may become even clearer, as shown in the table below:

TRAVEL AGENCY	
PRODUCTS	SERVICES
Brochures of tour operators Package holiday products Transport tickets (air, rail, ferry etc.) Foreign currency/bureau de change	Advice Information on transport and accommodation providers Insurance Advice on visa and legal requirements Car hire at destination Marketing and PR

◀ Travel agency products and services

Tourism products can come in three main types – package, independent and all-inclusive.

A **package** product is one made up of various components, such as travel, accommodation, attractions (through excursions) and could possibly include provision of leisure and recreation facilities at the accommodation site. All the various providers combine their products to form a complete package, put together by the tour operator, and marketed through travel agencies or direct to the consumer.

The **independent** product is one purchased by an individual, which may be an air or rail ticket to a particular destination, or the reservation of hotel or guest house accommodation for a specific period of time. It could also be that a tourist, while visiting a resort, requires catering products and so independently chooses the provider from the selection available. The transaction here is made between the independent traveller or tourist and the product provider – there is no middleman or intermediary, such as the travel agent or tour operator, involved. Another interpretation of an independent traveller may be one who buys a package of flights and car hire, with possibly one night's accommodation at the destination. Whilst in the destination country the traveller purchases accommodation and catering and visits attractions or sports and recreation facilities independently according to individual choice.

The **all-inclusive** product is where the transport, transfers, accommodation, meals, drinks and the use of all the facilities at the resort (such as water sports, gym or sports equipment, or ski equipment hire) are all included in the price of the holiday. It may also include some excursions within the holiday price which form part of the whole package. Whilst at the resort, which may be a large complex, the tourist is often required to provide some form of identification to ensure that only official guests are taking advantage of the all-inclusive offer. The tourist therefore only has to purchase additional excursions taken outside the holiday complex and any souvenirs or other products purchased either in shops at the complex or off-site. Cruise holidays are almost all-inclusive, as they include meals, accommodation and the services of staff, but do not include drinks purchased at the bar or dinner table, items purchased in on-board shops or excursions.

The **ancillary services** concern such things as **guiding services.** These may be provided by the attraction, such as museum guides, or local tour guides round a particular location (such as a city tour guide who knows the area very well and is probably local to the area). But guiding may also come in the form of tour directors or couriers on escorted coach tours. Their role is to ensure that the needs of the passengers are accommodated, give information on the places to be visited or area through which the tour is passing, and to sell any of the optional excursions which may be available whilst on the tour. An operator specialising in tours will normally state in the brochure whether the tour is fully escorted throughout by a specialised courier or whether the driver of the coach in a combined role undertakes this function.

Another ancillary service is **currency exchange**. This may be provided by the travel agency, the banks in an area, at the larger hotels or at specific bureaux de change. The rates are normally displayed according to whether the tourist is buying or selling the currency, and different rates given for notes and travellers' cheques. Usually four rates are displayed, the buy and sell rate for travellers' cheques, and the buy and sell rate for notes. Coins may be issued by exchangers, but rarely do they accept coins for exchange as the values tend to be low. A commission fee is normally charged for exchanging money into the local currency from foreign currency, and vice versa, and this rate can vary from one provider to another. The rates of exchange are taken from the daily financial press, so there can be fluctuations from one day to another. When travelling in the USA, visitors are often advised to carry travellers' cheques in American dollars, as these are accepted in shops, restaurants, attractions and hotels, often in preference to hard currency.

Marketing of tourism products may take place in various forms. Large travel agency chains may undertake their own marketing activities, promoting specific brochures, companies or specific services (such as commission-free currency exchange) on particular occasions. Tour operators also undertake their own marketing, through advertisements in various media, such as newspapers, television and magazines, but their aim is to promote the features and availability of specific products. Other forms of marketing may take place at trade or holiday fairs.

Trade fairs are aimed at buyers in the market. For example, a coach operator may visit a trade fair to negotiate with hotel and attraction providers in order to make up a package that would be sold to potential customers through the coach operator's brochure. Regional tourist boards or local authorities often exhibit in order to raise awareness of the facilities and attractions in their area and produce literature to support these products. This literature may also be available to potential individual customers who are considering visiting a locality and may be obtained through tourist information centre contacts.

Holiday fairs, on the other hand, are directed at the individual traveller, who may be able to make bookings whilst at the fair (often with an incentive discount), as well as receive information to peruse at leisure on the country, airline, accommodation or package. These holiday fairs tend to be held at times when the majority of potential travellers are considering their long vacation. In the UK this tends to be during the winter months, when the weather is cold or wet, and when people may be more willing to consider their holiday destinations to have something to look forward to.

Chapter 5: 'Marketing and promotion' looks in more detail at marketing in the industry.

The roles of tour operators and travel agents

Tour operators are the wholesalers of tourism products, in that they assemble the component parts of a holiday (i.e. travel, accommodation, transfers, excursions, facilities and other services). They buy in bulk from the providers of these travel services, such as hoteliers and airlines, and break this bulk down into separate packages which are then marketed to the consumer. This enables them to have **economies of scale**, as the more products they buy from the providers the better price they pay. They are probably able to obtain reduced rates for airline seats and hotel accommodation because they are buying in bulk and they undertake the responsibility for marketing the product. The airlines then have more guaranteed seat sales and the hotels have higher occupancy rates, which in turn keep the costs down to the provider. The scale of operations is so large that some of the largest tour operators virtually control the market price for packages. Some operators may also integrate vertically, and purchase airlines or hotels in order to maximise their economies of scale and also control the final product. Tour operators need to consider demand for holidays in specific seasons and may only offer certain packages for certain seasons. They need to consider the price the traveller is prepared to pay when compiling the package as well as the price of competitors for the same target group.

The method of marketing may be **direct selling** to the consumer, using various types of media (including press, television and brochures) and communication (internet, telephone etc.), or it may be through the **travel agencies** who act as the retail component in the chain of distribution. Figure 26 simplifies this.

Figure 26 ▶
Chain of distribution
for package holidays

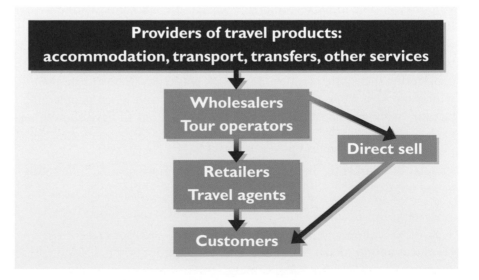

The total finished product is then sold at a specific price, which includes the costs of all the components, and may be for a package in the home country or for an international tour or holiday. There has been an increase in the number of packages sold direct to the consumer, particularly with the growth of the internet, which has benefits of direct sell in that the tour operators do not have to pay commission to the travel agents on the sales they generate. This can have the overall effect of reducing the price of the package holiday the tour operator can offer. Also some operators allow consumers to customise their holiday, by including an opportunity for extensions in a particular location or, on long-haul journeys, stop-overs in specific places. This results in tour operators being able to tailor-make a holiday to suit an individual client but still retain the business for the tour operator, and is therefore much more flexible.

In the UK there are generally four types of tour operator:
- **mass market operators** – such as Thomson, Airtours, Kuoni, Cosmos;
- **specialist operators** – such as Saga (specialising in holidays for over-50s), Voyages Jules Verne (selection of tours to specific areas for smaller intimate groups), Spirit of Adventure or PGL Adventure Holidays (activity and adventure holidays in more remote locations);
- **domestic operators** – those who specialise in holidays within the UK such as Highlife Breaks (travel and hotels in London, other cities and country houses);
- **incoming tour operators** – who provide tours for visitors from overseas in the UK, such as British Heritage Tours and Evans Tours.

Tour operators in the UK may belong to trade associations, which are designed not only to protect their members but also to guarantee certain standards of performance which can be expected by clients. Many specialist tour operators are members of AITO (Association of Independent Tour Operators), which is:

> dedicated to providing a quality product, personal service and choice to the consumer. The Association was established in 1976 ... and has come to be recognized as the official voice of the smaller or specialist tour operator whose views had seldom been represented or given due consideration by those who regulate the travel industry.
>
> Source: www.aito.co.uk

In the UK, incoming tour operators may well belong to BITOA (British Incoming Tour Operators Association). This is an independent organisation aiming to provide a forum for the exchange of information and ideas and to follow an accepted code of practice when dealing with other bodies in the UK with a common interest in tourism matters.

Activities

- Carry out research in your country to try and identify at least three tour operators in each category listed. From their promotional material or brochures establish if they belong to any trade organisations such as BITOA or AITO which operate in your country.
- If you have national trade organisations, what are their aims and how are these implemented?

These organisations also help to offer **consumer protection** by monitoring members and, through membership fees and bondings, support any tour operator who fails to provide the service. So if a member tour operator or travel agency fails financially customers who are currently away on holiday will be repatriated. Other forms of consumer protection concern areas such as health and safety in hotels, apartments, cruise ships and aircraft; the quality of bathing water and other environmental issues; plus protection of payments made by customers whether in deposits or final payments. The European Union Directives (legal procedures) set out procedures which must be followed by any operator or agency within the European Union area. But every country has its own legal requirements for consumer protection, and you will need to investigate those which apply in your home country.

Activity

Investigate the forms of consumer protection which tour operators and travel agencies must offer in your home country. This could relate to health and safety, package travel regulations, accommodation grading, and/or financial protection. Using the information collected (whether individually or in groups) prepare a guide which could be used by a travel agency or tour operator to reassure customers of the protection they would receive.

The functions of retail travel agents have been covered in Chapter 1 of this book, and this includes the selling of the tour operators' and providers' products, whether package holidays or air and rail tickets, or booking accommodation for customers. The products and services offered could include all or some of the following:

PRODUCTS	SERVICES
Overseas package tours	Advice on visa and passport applications
Short breaks in the home country	Guidance on suitability of product for customer and needs
'Flight only' sales	
Theatre bookings	Collection of deposits and final payments
Ferry bookings	Issue of brochures to suit needs
Activity and special interest holidays	Plan travel itineraries
Cruising holidays	Work out costings
Travel insurance	Issue tickets
Foreign exchange and travellers' cheques	Keep accounts
Hotel bookings	Book airport car parking spaces or car hire

◀ Products and services offered by retail travel agents

The main role of retail travel agents is to sell the products of the providers. For this they receive commission from the provider which in the UK could be approximately:

- package holidays   10 per cent
- airline tickets   7.5–9 per cent
- ferry bookings   9 per cent
- travellers' cheques   1 per cent
- travel insurance   35–40 per cent.

From this you will note that the selling of travel insurance is the biggest earner for the travel agent, which is often why customers are encouraged to purchase the insurance cover at the time of booking. However, many clients who travel frequently now have their own individual annual policies, thus reducing the demand at travel agencies. Some principals offer incentive commission, which can rise with the volume of sales. So if, for example, a travel agency sells its target of $50,000 of holidays with one company, it could earn $5,000 commission. If it exceeds that target, it may be offered 12.5 per cent commission on sales over $50,000.

This is one way of encouraging travel agencies to promote the products of a particular principal. Some agencies may be appointed 'sole agency' within a town or region to sell a particular principal's products, such as rail tickets. The rail company will only pay commission to the sole agency, and any other retail travel agencies in that area must purchase through this sole agency for their customers. The sole agency will obtain the maximum commission available, and pay the other travel agencies a maximum of say 7 per cent commission. The difference helps to pay the costs of the sole agency. This form of operation is called 'override commission', where the sole agency retains a small 'override' to cover its own costs.

Some retail travel agencies may have a **business travel** specialist, or even a business travel department, catering exclusively for the needs of corporate clients. The needs of the business client are often very different from those of the leisure tourist. Business clients usually have to use scheduled services rather than charter flights (due to the short notice for travel). Their needs in accommodation may be more business-oriented than those of the leisure traveller, as they may require access to a fax, modem points and office services such as photocopying. The value of the booking and respective commissions is so much higher for the business client that any extra effort needed to maintain business clients makes it beneficial to the travel agency.

Support facilities for travel and tourism

For tourism to be successful there must be some basic **infrastructure** in place. Infrastructure is the provision of utilities such as drainage, water supply, power cables, telecommunication links, as well as road, ports and/or airports. Basic infrastructure such as roads, ports and airports along with utilities is generally provided by public bodies, whether national or local governments or bodies reporting to government departments, such as tourism boards. The funds are provided through taxation of the population and the government or local authority designate the areas for

Figure 27 ▶
A travel agency promotion for additional services

Source: Lunn Poly

development through planning controls and regulations. Some areas may receive additional funding from external sources, such as the WTO (World Tourism Organisation) or United Nations Development Programme in order to develop their economic well-being or promote particular developments.

But the provision of facilities, such as accommodation, attractions, catering and entertainment, tends to be funded by private organisations and individuals, where the funding comes from personal capital or profits from other areas of the organisation. A hotel chain may have sufficient revenue available to develop accommodation in a particular resort area, or a private individual may open a restaurant in a locality which has a developing tourist market. A single visitor attraction may be of sufficient size to qualify as a destination in its own right, such as the Grand Canyon in America, the Egyptian Pyramids, The Great Wall of China, Disney World in Florida, Universal Studios in California, or a capital city with museums, theatres and historic buildings.

All of these compose multiple products, services and facilities, but the infrastructure is the basic transport connection, communication and utilities provision. If a resort is being developed, potential tourists must be able to reach the destination, businesses at the destination will need to be able to communicate with other external providers and suppliers, and the destination area must have basic hygiene facilities in place. One of the problems when Turkey was increasing its tourist numbers was that there was inadequate infrastructure in place to support the numbers of tourists. The airports could not cope with the baggage handling or volume of flights, the roads were inadequate for transporting visitors to their destinations and the water and drainage facilities could not cope with the additional numbers. Initially this resulted in some health scares when visitors contracted diseases due to contamination, and some accommodation was not completed in time for visitor arrivals. The result was that the area suffered adverse publicity and a reduction in visitor numbers. The government and tour operators had to co-operate to improve the infrastructure before promoting resorts further.

When the public and private sectors co-operate to market a developing destination, then the necessary planning and regulatory controls and infrastructure should be in place. However problems arise when a private developer wishes to increase capacity in order to improve profits without the supporting provision of transport and communication links.

Without planning and regulatory controls, it is possible that a resort may become overcrowded or over-developed, thus spoiling the initial attraction to that resort.

Increases in passenger numbers have affected airport provision with many international hub airports now requiring additional terminals to cater for the flying public, whether arrivals, departure or transit passengers. The sizes of aircraft and length of runways needed also affect the infrastructure provision. A regional airport may only be able to cater for smaller planes but will still need access roads for potential passengers and cargo (including aviation fuel and catering supplies for in-flight meals and cafeterias in the terminals) without affecting the normal traffic in an area. Those passengers will expect to have services such as toilets, catering, newspapers and books or other travel goods available. This needs to be planned in any development stage. Those resorts and destinations which rely on ferry and cruise traffic will also need the same provision of basic infrastructure and access as airports. To quote the WTO:

> Travel and tourism stimulates enormous investments in new infrastructure, most of which helps to improve the living conditions of local residents as well as tourists. Tourism development projects often include airports, roads, marinas, sewage systems, water treatment plants, restoration of cultural monuments, museums and nature interpretation centres.

Development of infrastructure will influence the development of tourism in an area, and the two are inseparably linked – the one will not happen without the other being developed or in place.

Type and range of accommodation available

Accommodation is usually classified into two main segments: serviced and self-catering.

Serviced accommodation relates to the provision of other services in addition to an overnight stay, and this would include such things as catering, housekeeping, valet services and possibly even games rooms, health facilities and other social entertainment areas. So within this category there is a wide range of providers – including hotels, bed and breakfasts, guesthouses, inns, youth hostels and farm guesthouses.

Self-catering or self-serviced accommodation provides only the overnight accommodation with the tourist catering for all other needs independently, including food and servicing of the room. In this category, the following are some of the examples available – villas, apartments, time-share apartments, rented houses and cottages, chalets, boats, college or university rooms out of termtime, second homes and home 'swaps'.

The distinction between serviced and self-catering providers is not always clear, as some of the latter now offer additional facilities for their overnight occupants. One example of this could be Center Parcs holiday villages in Europe, where holidaymakers are offered a wide range of sports facilities, eating places, shopping opportunities and a child-minding service along with self-catering villa accommodation.

Many countries operate a grading system for hotels and self-catering so that the tourist can gauge the level of service and facilities offered. As an example, the English Tourism Council uses the following system:

◀ Key to the English Tourism Council's grading system

Hotels	*****	Graded by a star system ranging from one to five stars, with the higher numbers denoting progressively higher standards and a wider range of facilities and services.
Guesthouses and bed and breakfasts	♦♦♦♦♦	The diamond ratings reflect visitor expectations of this sector, so a higher number of diamonds denotes progressively higher levels of quality and customer care.
Self-catering	🔑🔑🔑🔑🔑	Graded by keys, where one key means there is the minimum size of unit (at least one double or twin bedroom) dining and cooking facilities, refrigerator. More keys indicate more facilities.
Holiday parks	*****	This shows the quality rating of holiday parks, touring parks and camping parks. The higher number of stars indicate more facilities.

Activity

For your own area, whether region or town, investigate the accommodation provided for tourists and categorise by type (serviced and self-catering). Identify the grading categories used in your area and list the accommodation by rating. From your national tourist board, establish the grading categories used and compare two types of accommodation in each category according to the facilities offered.

The majority of accommodation providers throughout the world are commercial organisations, whose aim is to make a profit. There are many international chains of hotel operators – e.g. Holiday Inn, Marriott, Sheraton, Ibis, Hilton, Novotel – some of whom operate hotels branded according to the level of facilities offered. Marriott, for example, have luxury hotels carrying the 'Marriott' prefix to the hotel name, but they also operate 'Courtyard by Marriott' (offering medium-range facilities and rooms at a lower price than the major Marriotts) and Fairview Inns (which offer simpler accommodation and often have limited breakfast facilities only).

Other commercial operators may only own one or two accommodation outlets and in the case of farmhouse bed and breakfasts this may be a way of providing additional income to the basic business of farming. In some socialist countries there are joint-venture operations, where the private organisations and the national government negotiate to build accommodation in order to develop tourism.

The **scale of investment** will be related to the size of the business on the basis that the more one invests, the more the owner hopes to make in profits in return. Large chains obviously will have greater funds available for investment than small single owner businesses but all are competing for the same tourists. Each hopes to meet the demands of individual tourists by the provision of services to meet those individuals' needs. Some people prefer small and 'friendly' hotels, whereas others want more luxurious surroundings with a wider range of facilities.

But all aim to achieve **economies of operation,** whether in staffing costs, maintenance or purchase of raw materials such as foodstuffs and housekeeping items. The larger the facility, the more leverage they may have with suppliers and the more able they are to buy in bulk leading to economies of scale. A smaller operator may only purchase the minimum requirements at any one time, so would have to pay the market price at that time, and may not be able to take advantage of bulk purchases.

Occupancy rates is the generic term used to describe the percentage of rooms occupied over a period of time, say a year or a season. Accommodation providers set themselves a minimum occupancy rate when preparing financial budgets for their operation. If the hotel does not reach this minimum occupancy rate, then basic costs will not be covered. Any excess over this minimum occupancy rate will lead to profits and may help to fund additional facilities in the establishment. In order to reach occupancy rates, any accommodation provider will need to market and promote the facility and may be prepared to offer special discounts and promotions in order to attract new customers to meet/exceed budget figures.

The **facilities offered for leisure and business tourists** differ, as the needs of the customers vary. A business tourist would expect sufficient space in the room to carry out work duties, along with possibly telecommunications links via modem and telephone points. Supporting office services may also be required, such as photocopying, fax or mail collection/storage and conference facilities. A business tourist may also require access to food at unsocial hours due to his or her itinerary, so the accommodation provider may have to provide 24-hour room service, or at least up to midnight and from early morning. The leisure tourist would not need these same facilities, but large city centre hotels may have to cater for both types of tourists so will need to provide some of the facilities to cater for the needs of both. Leisure tourists may be more interested in recreational facilities at a hotel, such as swimming pool, gym, games area or outdoor sports provision.

Activity

Visit one of the larger hotels in your area and find out about its facilities. Establish whether the market is largely for the leisure or business tourist and analyse whether the needs of that tourist are met. Undertake some research amongst the customers of the hotel to identify any gaps in the provision and prepare a report on your findings.

Public transport provision

When tourists visit a location, they are concerned not only with the connecting transport links to the location but also with the quality and accessibility of local public transport. If a tourist arrives by air, and is not provided with transfers to the accommodation by the tour operator, there must be some provision for their transfer to the destination.

Airports naturally tend to be outside built-up areas or some distance from city centres so there need to be connecting services available. Signs are provided directing arriving passengers to available services, but if these are not visual (i.e. illustrative) then the visitor may not understand them.

The main services provided from airports are **taxis or shuttle buses**, which are obviously going to use the roads, but these may be expensive, particularly if the airport is a distance from the city centre. Some major airports now have express link coach services to city centres or to other airports (such as the Airport Link service connecting London's four major airports – Heathrow, Gatwick, Luton and Stansted). However, if the roads in the area are liable to be congested, then the journey time may be longer than anticipated, making connections more difficult.

Alternative forms of transport could be **rail or underground services**, connecting the airport to the rail or underground network, but these do not always operate 24 hours a day. One of the requirements when building new airports has been the necessity to consider passenger numbers and the most economic method of transporting large numbers of people. Rail services (or underground) are considered the most cost-effective method, and if stations can be located in close proximity to the airport terminal, more people could be encouraged to use this facility, thus reducing congestion on the roads.

If an airport has more than one terminal, then the airport authorities consider **integrated rapid transit systems**, whether by monorail or underground, to enable easy movement of passengers. The system used at Chicago O'Hare Airport in the USA, where there are currently at least four large terminal buildings, is an automated transfer train system. Trains run every two or three minutes and interior information systems indicate which terminal the train will stop at next and which airlines use that terminal. The platforms are designed with glass walls with sets of opening doors at certain points and the trains stop only at those points. Doors open on one side for passengers to disembark, close, then open on the opposite side for embarking passengers. This enables a speedy transit of passengers who are all moving in the same direction, so there is less likelihood of injury and no delay loading and unloading. Guidebooks for destinations often provide detailed information on access to and from the airport with some indication of costs. Examples of some are given below:

> **Ground transport:** Airport terminals provide a cheap bus ride into town at regular timings, throughout the night if the airport is a busy one. Airport bus services exist at most smaller places. You are also

assured of finding taxis and motor rickshaws. Taxi-runs from the airport are on set fares which naturally vary from airport to airport. Convenient pre-paid taxi services operate in Delhi and Bombay.

Source: *Berlitz Country Guide to India*

Taxi: $30 plus tolls and tip. Take only a licensed cab from the official ranks.
Bus: Carey Airport Express Coach ... about every 30 minutes. Gray Line Air Shuttle ... Shared minibus to any location.
Helicopter: Helicopter Flight Services ... about $600 into the 34th Street heliport for up to four people.

Source: *AA City Pack*, New York, JFK Airport

Rome's airports are Leonardo da Vinci (Fiumicino) and Ciampino. Transfers: from Leonardo da Vinci the most hassle-free way of getting into town is the 30-minute journey by metered taxi (allow two hours at peak times). Trains link the airport directly with Stazione Termini (a 30-minute journey, one train an hour most of the day); and Stazione Tiburtina (a 45-minute trip every 20 minutes from 6am to 1am). On the latter line you can alight at Stazione Ostiense and change to taxi, bus or Metro. From Ciampino there is a bus service (ACOTRAL or ATAC) to Anagnina Metro station (service from 5.30 am, every half hour until 10.30 pm). From there the Metro (Line A) heads towards Termini.

Source: *Traveller's Rome*, AA Thomas Cook

Rail services are available within most countries for tourists to use. The advantage of rail over self-drive is the opportunity to enjoy the scenery and observe local people in their working habitats. However, rail services vary considerably from country to country as regards frequency, reliability, cleanliness and supporting services. Some are extremely efficient (for example, in Japan and Switzerland), others are less reliable. Stations are normally fairly centrally placed in towns and cities, so can be more convenient to access, but the services may be local or express. Local trains tend to stop at most of the stations on the planned journey, whereas express services either go from one large town or city to another with no stops between, or specified stops at some distance apart.

Rail services have the advantage of being able to move large numbers of people effectively and are not normally subject to the same level of congestion as road traffic. As mentioned previously, rail can be overland or underground, and many large cities now have some form of underground or metro system operating to enable high volumes of users to access points in the city quickly. The cost of services varies enormously both within and between countries. Government-operated systems tend to be relatively cheap, but those operated by commercial organisations can prove more expensive.

Within regions, **buses or coaches** are a popular form of transport and again operate on a timetabled schedule, though reliability and frequency may not always match the quoted timetable. Some large cities, such as St Petersburg, Rome, Singapore, Orlando, have extended buses, which are the size of two single-decker coaches joined with a turntable platform (bridged over with tubing) in the centre (to improve flexibility and mobility) – often called 'bendy buses'. These are able to transport large numbers of people and often have priority over other road traffic so can be very economical and efficient forms of transport.

Transport is not always solely provided by the government of a country. Some sections may be provided by independent operators. But the intention is to provide an effective public transport system enabling locals and visitors to reach their destinations. National transport systems, such as rail or express coach services, tend to operate over greater distances. Once at a destination, tourists tend to use the local transport available, whether underground, metrolink, bus, coach or taxi. Factors affecting their choice would be ease of use, cost, time of day and availability in the locality. Altogether, transport services form a vital support facility for the travel and tourism industry.

Worldwide transport in relation to major international routes

Air transport

Air traffic is generally divided into three categories:
- domestic flights
- international scheduled flights
- international chartered flights.

We will look at these in turn.

Domestic services are those that refer to travel within one country, whereas international services represent travel between different countries. A country may have many smaller regional airports which handle domestic services, but only a limited number which handle international services. These latter act as 'hub' airports not only for passengers connecting from domestic to international flights, but also for those incoming passengers who need to change aircraft or airline for their onward journey.

If we look at the map of the world in Figure 9 (see Chapter 2, p.32), and compare the size of the continents, it is easy to understand why some countries may have more than one major international airport.

Using the USA as an example, the major international carriers into and from the area would tend to use one of the major international airports, though other airports may also receive international passengers. The list below shows the main hub airports (giving their airport code) with examples of some of the airlines which use them:

CITY	AIRPORT	AIRLINES
New York	JFK (NYJ), La Guardia (NYL) or Newark (NYE) Airports	JFK serves 59 international airlines including United Airlines, Alitalia, Aeroflot, British Airways, Qantas Singapore Airlines, Cathay Pacific, Air India, Air Afrique, Lufthansa
Chicago	O'Hare International Airport (CHO)	American Airlines Delta Airlines British Airways
Los Angeles	LA International Airport (LAX)	British Airways Cathay Pacific Singapore Airlines Continental Japan
Atlanta	Atlanta International (ATL)	18 international airlines, including Delta Airways American Airlines British Airways

◄ Main hub airports of the USA

By comparison, Heathrow (LHR) in London UK serves over 90 airlines, 62 million passengers in 2000, travelling to approximately 200 destinations on only 2 runways but using 4 terminals. It is one of the world's busiest international airports and the second busiest cargo port. It has been regarded as 'the hub of the aviation world' according to the British Airports Authority.

Scheduled services are those that operate to a published timetable on clearly defined routes and under government licence. Even if there are no passengers, the service must run and these tend to be used primarily by business travellers because they are prepared to pay premium fares for the extra convenience, reliability and flexibility of transfer to other transport at the destination. Many governments still fund their national airlines, for example Air India, Air France and Singapore Airlines, but there has been a general move away from state ownership towards private sector operation or joint operations between the private and public sectors. Sometimes, this has been seen as giving unfair advantages to the state-owned airline as national prestige rather than profit is seen as the major priority of the airline's operation. Since they receive subsidy from the government, they can offer unfair competition to the privately owned airlines for the same target market. The size of planes and corresponding number of seats often reflect the demand for that particular route or the frequency of the scheduled flight operation. If an airline has several flights a day to a particular destination, it may be more economical to operate small–medium sized aircraft (carrying 100–150 passengers) on that route for some of those flights. However, if an airline is only flying to a major international destination say twice a week, then the size of aircraft used is probably going to be much larger (such as those able to carry more than 300 passengers).

Figure 28 ▶
Boeing 747

Source: Boeing 747 website www.boeing.com

Charter services, on the other hand, are used largely by the package holiday industry, which can represent a major proportion of passenger traffic in many countries where there is an established outbound tourism market. These services are generally cheaper than scheduled flights and operators aim to fill as many seats as possible and will only offer the flight if they can guarantee a minimum number of passengers to break even. This breakeven figure may be as high as 85 to 90 per cent capacity, and only after reaching this volume of sales will the airline provider make a profit on the flight. You will find more details on scheduled and charter flight operations in Chapter 6, pp. 138–9, where travel arrangements are covered.

The growth in air transport has developed enormously since the end of the Second World War and airline fleet growth, according to Boeing:

> was dominated by airlines adjusting fleet mix, route development and traffic to the new availability of big, efficient, twin-aisle airplanes. Since 1985 airlines have been able to choose from a complete spectrum of airplane sizes for all but the longest markets. Thus, fleet additions since 1985 largely represent continuing needs and are not distorted by a major re-equipment cycle and new airplane capabilities. Air travel has doubled since 1985.

> Annual average growth of 5.1% per year varied by region. Some regions have shown annual growth as high as 11% while others fell below 4%. History shows that where economies grow, travel grows. Growth is somewhat faster where the initial travel is unusually low for the level of wealth.

It is anticipated that the world stock of aeroplanes will increase greatly, from 13,670 in 1999 to approximately 31,755 in 2019 - the number will have more than doubled over a 20-year period. However, the adjustments to fleet mix are expected to change to meet changing demands in economic growth. It is projected that there will be a small decline, of around 1%, in 747s and larger planes and that the number of single-aisle planes, including larger regional jets, will decline by 10%, from 67% to 57%. The biggest growth will be in the smaller regional jet sector of the market (planes with up to 150 seats). This is forecast to grow from 7% of the world air fleet in 1999 to 15% in 2019. These jets need shorter runways, fewer cabin staff and can operate more economically over shorter-distance routes. The twin-aisle, intermediate-size aeroplanes sector is likely to gain 3% of world fleet size. These projected figures will enable airlines to operate within a competitive environment, in order to meet the growing needs of the travelling public.

Using the diagram below as an example, it is possible to see how world economic growth has affected international passenger demand on scheduled services from 1983 to 2000. The growth in travel has broadly reflected economic growth, with deficit figures in 1991 at the time of the Gulf War.

Figure 29 ▶

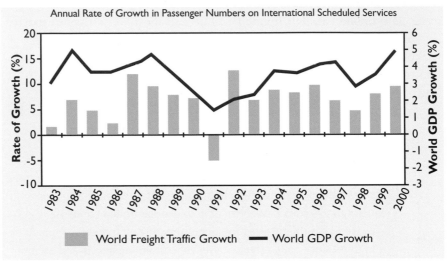

Source: IATA website www.iata.org

Activity

Identify the major international airports in your area of the world. Produce a table showing the international airport code and list the airlines using those airports. Search the internet to get fuller details of estimated passenger growth for one of those airports and identify how it plans to meet that demand (e.g. build more runways, increase terminal size, improve infrastructure etc.).

The regulation of air traffic may be undertaken on a national and international basis. National governments may stipulate the standards of safety, airport management, operation of airlines as regards routes, competition along with other supplementary regulations. International regulations tend to fall under the remit of **IATA (International Air Transport Association)** whose mission statement includes the following clauses:

- the collective voice of the world's fastest growing transport sector – which in turn is part of the world's largest industry – travel and tourism;
- to represent and serve the airline industry;
- ensure that people, freight and mail can move around the vast global airline network as easily as if they were on a single airline;
- that members' aircraft can operate safely, securely, efficiently and economically under clearly defined and understood rules;
- allows airlines to operate more efficiently and offers joint ways to exploit opportunities, reduce costs and solve problems;
- provides a useful means for governments to work with airlines and draw on their experience and expertise. Industry working standards are developed within IATA.

The standards and procedures developed have included multilateral interline traffic agreements (whereby some 300 airlines will accept each other's passengers and cargo traffic on a reciprocal basis), standards for carrying disabled passengers, dangerous goods regulations, a WorldTracer system for lost or misdirected goods and items, and automated ticket and fraud prevention.

Regulations are also in place controlling noise and other pollution caused by increased air traffic, particularly concerning residential areas surrounding airports and the safety of aircraft in flight path areas. Some countries operate regulations controlling the number of flights to particular destinations and oversee or manage airline dominance to or from specific destinations. **Deregulation** of air travel has increased the level of competition between airlines and this has helped to keep fares low on an increasingly large number of routes, both domestic and international.

Activity

Investigate any regulations your government has made concerning air traffic operations and if there are any proposals to restrict the number of airlines using your international airports.

The **Air Transport Action Group** (ATAG), is:

> an independent coalition of organisations from throughout the air transport industry uniting to press for economically beneficial aviation capacity improvements in an environmentally friendly manner.
>
> Source: Air Transport Action Group, 1997

The ATAG has produced various papers on growth and constraints in air traffic development. One which may be worth further investigation by students can be found on www.atag.org/asia.index and concerns developments in Asia and the Pacific region. This document highlights the fact that air traffic grew at an annual average rate of 10.1 per cent between 1985 and 1995 and is anticipated to grow approximately 7.4 per cent between 1995 and 2010. The points raised highlight the need for considered development of infrastructure to cater for this increased demand and the effects on local economies.

Sea transport

Most nations of the world have at least one major port, largely for the shipping of cargo but often also acting as a major transit point for passenger shipping. In this section you need to be able to identify the main ports in the world as well as any international passenger ferry routes. You will also find more information on types of sea transport and some identified ferry routes in Chapter 6: 'Travel organisation'. There has been a sharp increase in the volume of cruise tourism during the past decade with the result that providers of cruise ships are now operating very large (with 2,500 passengers or more) ships with a much broader range of facilities on board to meet this increased demand. Most major cruise shipping lines have a base port, and these have the dock capacity to cope with the supply and loading of stock needed to cater for huge numbers of people and the infrastructure (i.e. roads and railways) to enable passengers and freight to reach the ship.

The following table shows some of the major ports from which cruises depart:

Major cruise departure ports ▶

COUNTRY	PORT	DESTINATION
United States of America	Miami, Florida	Caribbean Bahamas Bermuda
	Los Angeles	Hawaiian Islands Australia

→ **(contd)**

COUNTRY	PORT	DESTINATION
Italy	Genoa or Venice	Mediterranean Croatia
Greece	Athens (Piraeus)	Greek Islands Baltic Sea
United Kingdom	Southampton	Atlantic crossings Atlantic islands North European capitals Mediterranean South and North America
Singapore	Singapore	Indian Ocean Malaysia Pacific Islands Indonesia Australia
Argentina	Buenos Aires	Caribbean Islands Chile Uruguay Falkland Islands
Australia	Sydney	New Zealand Philippines Singapore South Pacific Indonesia Tasmania
Canada	Vancouver	Alaska California, USA
China	Hong Kong	Japan Chinese Islands Sydney South Pacific
Turkey	Istanbul	Black Sea Turkish coast and Greece

International ferry routes may depart from the major ports listed above, but also operate from other ports in many countries of the world. Ferry journeys tend to be shorter than those undertaken by cruise ships. In the North Sea area there are various crossing routes, such as Hull, UK to Rotterdam, The Netherlands, Oslo, Sweden and Copenhagen, Denmark; or Newcastle, UK to Bergen, Norway. There are also regular routes across the English Channel to France and Spain; routes across the Irish Sea between the UK and Northern Ireland or the Republic of Ireland; plus routes from Scotland, UK to the various islands off the mainland. In the Mediterranean, there are ferry routes between Marseilles, France and Algeria, Sardinia and the Balearic Islands of Spain. There are also routes from various Italian ports such as Genoa to the western Mediterranean Islands; Bari or Brindisi and Venice to the Greek Islands, Albania and Croatia, as well as Piraeus, Greece to the various Greek Islands in the Aegean Sea and Mediterranean. Moving east, ferries operate between Singapore and Malaya or the Indonesian Islands of Borneo, Bali and Lombok and regular ferries between the various groups of islands in the Pacific, such as Hawaii, Polynesia, Solomon Islands and Vanuatu.

The difference between ferries and cruise routes is that the former run to a scheduled timetable, which may be subject to prevailing weather conditions. Passengers are able to book ahead for a particular crossing and date and providing they arrive at the point in suitable time for departure can make the crossing. Some ferries operate car and cargo services in addition to foot passenger traffic, which is vital for the transporting of goods between countries. Cruise ships on the other hand operate on an advertised route on specific dates and once joining the ship the package commences with the ports of call as part of the selling point for that particular voyage. Cargo vehicles and cars are not usually accommodated and any shore excursions are organised by the cruise operator.

Some ferry routes may be operated by different carriers, and the intending passengers must select their carrier and travel with that carrier only. This means that there is price competition between the various carriers, with each promoting the features of their ships that might attract particular groups of tourists. To be cost-effective, ferry providers aim for maximum capacity as the fares charged must cover the costs of services and crew over a period of time. There are peak travelling times such as during major holiday seasons when early booking is necessary to guarantee space on board. Most ferry journeys tend to be three to four nights maximum but some may only be short crossings of up to one hour. The longer the crossing time, the more expensive for the passenger.

There is more detail on types of ferries and cruises in Chapter 6: Travel organisation later in this book and you are advised to study this in order to meet the criteria for the completion of the Core Module.

Rail and road transport

When discussing the infrastructure of a country earlier in this chapter, there has been some coverage of the importance of rail and road transport in the travel and tourism industry. However, it is important to add to this the need for **international rail travel**, where nations co-operate to provide an integrated rail service across large land masses. An example of this would be Europe, where trains leaving from Paris, France, for example, may pass through Switzerland on their way to Rome or Venice in Italy. They also pass through Holland, Belgium and Germany on their way to Moscow or St Petersburg in Russia. They will stop at certain specified stations en route, but as they cross national boundaries there may be some passport checks. Passengers would be advised if visas were needed and may be required to produce one as proof of entry to a country at the time of purchasing a ticket. Other countries that operate international or trans-continental rail routes are those between various countries in southern Africa, such as from Cape Town, through the Orange Free State to Lesotho, Swaziland, Mozambique, Botswana or Zimbabwe; or the East–West Africa crossing through Angola, Zaire, Zambia and Tanzania.

America has two main cross-continent lines, with the United States system being operated by Amtrak (the main passenger and cargo operator) and in Canada by Canrail. Both of these operators provide a variety of rail pass enabling travel within a specific region of the country which can be pre-purchased by the tourist. Prices vary, with tickets for travel at off-peak times sometimes costing less than half the price of a pass enabling travel at peak times.

Some of the rail journeys can be undertaken as specialist travel, such as the Blue Train in South Africa, the Trans-Siberian Express from Moscow to China, or the Orient Express from London, UK or Paris, France to Venice, Italy. However, any train travelling on an intercontinental rail route would normally be on a scheduled service and the rail lines between the countries must be of the same gauge or width consistently. One of the difficulties on the Trans-Siberian Express is that when the train reaches the Chinese border, all the coaches have to be mechanically lifted from the wheels on the Chinese side to those on the Russian side as the tracks are not the same width. This can add some time to the overall journey. Better co-operation between countries may have prevented that, but each country is free to choose its own system.

In order to run cost-effective railways, each country or operator must undertake the marketing necessary to attract the passengers in sufficient volume to cover the basic costs and hopefully earn sufficient profits to reinvest in the rolling stock needed to maintain the standards of the railways. Japanese and Swiss railways are famous for their punctuality, cleanliness and efficiency, whereas other countries, such as India, may operate a punctual service but with less modern rolling stock.

Road transport has been discussed in earlier chapters in relation to tourism providers and there is some additional detail in Chapter 6 on 'Travel organisation'. But it must not be forgotten how important road transport and the supporting infrastructure of roads, bridges and tunnels is to the effectiveness of a nation's provision.

Many developed countries have built motorways (sometimes called expressways or autobahns). These are highways having three or four lanes of traffic in each direction and interchanges at specified points where traffic can switch from the motorway network to the other road system of the country. These are supposed to offer quicker, safer routes of travel and be able to carry large numbers of vehicles over long distances through rural areas, thus cutting down on urban pollution. When a motorway travels through different nations, there will be passport and visa controls, where the traveller must produce documents to prove identity and goods carriage.

Some motorways require tolls or fees to be paid – this money goes to the government or operating company to help fund the maintenance and improvement of roads. Car travellers need to be aware of the types of costs of these tolls when budgeting for their journey. Also along the motorway routes there may be areas for drivers to take a break from their journey (stretch their legs, eat meals or take refreshments, and toilet facilities). These service areas provide the basic facilities and some even have shops, bank terminals or ATMs, telephones and amusement areas to encourage further spending.

Away from the motorway networks and in other less-developed countries there will be some infrastructure of roads, most of which are hard surfaced with tarmacadam or asphalt. However, others may be less commonly used or badly eroded and the driver has to travel on sand, soil or through rough terrain. For some tourists this could be an adventure, but for the efficient mass movement of tourists, better provision should be made through government expenditure. Without the necessary infrastructure to support the development of tourism, the potential for economic growth in an area is damaged.

This section will be tested alongside the other three sections which make up the Core Module for the qualification by an externally set and assessed examination. The activities which follow will provide practice for the type of activities involved in the examination.

Extension Activities

1 Explain the differences between a package and an independent tourism product.
2 Why do different tourism product providers combine to market a 'tour' or 'package'?
3 Describe the operating characteristics and role of a travel agent.
4 What important features of infrastructure are necessary to the development of a tourist resort?
5 Select one large and one small accommodation provider in your locality. Describe the features of each and its target market. Compare the economies of operation of the two providers.
6 Select one continent from the world map and identify the major air and sea transport hubs. Explain why these may be important for the development of inbound tourism.

5 Marketing and promotion

Learning outcomes

In this chapter you will look at the principles of marketing and promotion and at the ways in which marketing and promotion are used within the travel and tourism industry. By the end of this chapter, you should be able to:

- recognise why marketing and promotion are important to travel and tourism organisations
- describe the main marketing techniques used in the industry
- identify the different market segments targeted by travel and tourism providers
- explain how different products cater for different market segments
- identify and explain the difference between products and services
- understand how these products and services have been developed
- identify a range of common pricing policies
- identify and explain the factors that determine pricing strategies
- explain the factors that influence the selection of a location for travel and tourism facilities
- understand the distribution channels that operate to ensure that travel and tourism products and/or services are made available to customers
- identify the main methods of promotion used
- explain the factors to consider when producing promotional materials

This chapter covers Optional Module 5252: Marketing and Promotion.

Travel and tourism organisations provide products and services for their customers. This concept was fully explored in the previous chapter (on 'Travel and tourism products and services'), and you should by now have a good understanding of the differences between products and services and how they contribute to the total travel and tourism experience of customers.

This chapter examines the way in which products and services are made available to customers within both commercial and non-commercial settings. It provides an opportunity to investigate reasons why organisations allocate large budgets to the process of marketing. It also gives an in-depth analysis of the range of marketing methods employed by travel and tourism providers, including the development of an effective marketing mix.

Role and function of marketing and promotion

We have already identified the fact that travel and tourism is a large, diverse global industry. **Marketing and promotion** play a significant role in allowing the large number of providers to raise awareness of their products and services amongst potential customers. Providers operate within a highly competitive market, with public, private and voluntary sector organisations vying for business, attempting to lure customers to use their products and services.

There are four main functions of marketing in the industry:
- to create a competitive advantage
- to increase sales and profitability
- to enhance the image of the organisation or product
- to improve customer satisfaction.

We will look at each of these in turn.

Competitive advantage
Those organisations with the greatest share of the market for any given product or service are described as market leaders, as they have successfully attracted a larger number of customers than their rivals. They have achieved a competitive advantage. This is particularly important in an industry which is dominated by private enterprise, each organisation needing to make a profit to remain in business.

Increased sales/usage/profitability
This links back to the concept of increasing the size of the customer base in an attempt to boost sales by both volume and value. Profit-seeking organisations aim to increase their profits; non-profit-seeking outfits aim to increase the number of users. Like any other business, travel and tourism organisations need to generate a sales income in order to survive.

Positive organisational and product image
Customers use the products and services of those organisations that they perceive to offer value for money and quality. Thus, an aim of marketing

is to ensure that the customer receives a positive image of the organisation and the products it offers.

Customer satisfaction

Chapter 3 on 'Customer care and working procedures' has already examined the importance of customer satisfaction as a determining factor in the success of an organisation. If the products and services that are offered are catered specifically to the needs of customers, then those customers are likely to show loyalty to that organisation by returning for repeat business.

Activities

- What is the main purpose behind a privately owned inbound tour operator marketing its products and services?
- How does this differ from the main purpose of a Tourist Information Centre trying to promote its services?
- Which purpose would both of these organisations have in common?

The main marketing and promotion techniques used in travel and tourism

In order to be able to set targets for future performance and improvement, any business venture must be certain of the market in which it operates. It needs to identify its main competitors and clearly understand the customers at whom the products and services are being targeted. This is particularly true of the travel and tourism industry, which has a customer focus, and where market forces change rapidly. The main method used to examine the current position of the market and the potential variations in the demand for and supply of products and services is market research.

Market research is the systematic collection and collation of data relating to consumer habits, wants and needs. Organisations are then able to use the information, which is extracted and analysed from the data, to inform future business decisions. There are two main types of research: primary marketing research and secondary marketing research.

Primary or **field** research involves the organisation and its customers in a first-hand research exercise. This can take the form of a **questionnaire**, which is passed to the customer to fill in. **Telephone surveys** are where an employee makes telephone contact with an existing or potential customer to ask questions relating to the products and services currently on offer. **Face-to-face interviews** are usually conducted at the facility, with a member of staff asking customers direct questions.

Secondary or **desk** research often results from the organisation using existing research findings conducted by a third party or data from the organisation's own records. **Internal sources** of secondary research data may include customer databases at a travel and tourism facility which detail the number of times a customer has used the products over a given period. Other data might outline the total sales value and volume during an accounting period. **External sources** of secondary research data can include government-produced statistics on visitor numbers, visitor spend, most popular attractions, etc., or industry-based data on reservations, occupancy rates etc. These data are often spread over a larger area than individual companies can usually use for their own research.

Primary research allows data to be collected of both a quantitative and qualitative nature. Quantitative data can be measured by frequency, cost and number of times visited and allows patterns and trends in consumer habits to be analysed graphically. Qualitative data relate to consumer preferences and opinions and are generated through the use of open questions, attracting a variety of responses. It is more difficult to represent in graph form. Secondary research tends to be of a quantitative nature, based on gathered statistics.

Activities

- Visit your local library and identify the range of secondary research sources that are available related to the study of travel and tourism markets.
- Design a brief questionnaire to use on visitors to your area, to find out their opinions of the existing attractions. Use the findings to consider improvements that could be made in tourism provision.

Marketing analysis tools

There is a wide variety of complex marketing analysis tools that have been developed by marketing experts. These marketing tools enable organisations to assess their place in the market and establish future improvements to products and services to enhance the company's market position. Two of these tools in particular are used by travel and tourism organisations in assessing market position. Both are known by their acronyms: SWOT and PEST.

The initial letter from each of four factors is taken to form the acronym **SWOT**:

Strengths of the market position
Weaknesses
Opportunities
Threats.

It is often presented as a SWOT box – a table showing each of the headings (see Figure 30). SWOT is widely used in many business contexts. Looking at each heading in turn, the organisation analyses the internal strengths and weaknesses of their operation, and then the external factors that present opportunities and threats to market proposals.

Similarly, the initial letter from each of four different influences on the market are taken to form the acronym **PEST**:

Political influences
Economic
Social
Technological.

This is often presented as a PEST circle (see Figure 31), with each influence heading a sector of the circle. It is used to examine a number of external influences that may impact on existing products or potential market proposals.

Activity

Select a travel and tourism organisation with which you are familiar. Use the tools below to conduct both a SWOT analysis and a PEST analysis of their current market position.

Figure 30 ▶
SWOT box (left)

Figure 31 ▶
PEST circle (right)

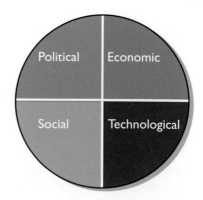

The **marketing mix** has been described by many as getting the right PRODUCT to the right people, at the right PRICE, at the right PLACE, using the right PROMOTIONAL methods. This is often known as the '4 Ps' for the marketing mix. Every organisation has to select the most effective combination of factors to determine how their product will be marketed, how the price will be set, and at whom the product will be aimed. These considerations form the basis of this optional module, when examining the way in which this mix is put together for certain travel and tourism organisations.

Market segmentation and targeting

Market segmentation is the process through which organisations can carefully target individual products and services at specific sections of the population. Market research enables the characteristics of potential customers to be identified, and allows the total market to be broken down into subsections, or segments. The benefits of this are twofold: the organisation can focus its marketing efforts only on those customers who are most likely to buy or use the products on offer. Second, the customer benefits from being on the receiving end of marketing activities of relative interest to them.

There are three main ways in which target markets can be segmented:
- *by geographical location* – certain travel and tourism products and services will be of specific interest only to those within a defined location, be it for cultural or access reasons.
- *using demographics* – age, gender and levels of disposable income are all used to determine the characteristics of a target market. There is a complex set of social grade classifications used to describe individuals by their income level. Examples of some of these grades are:
  Group A – upper middle class, higher-level professionals and managers such as barristers and surgeons;
  Group B – middle class, intermediate-level managers and professionals including teachers and doctors;
  Group E – those at the lowest level of subsistence, including those on low or very limited incomes, such as pensioners, the unemployed and students.
  (Many organisations have moved away from using these classifications, as they are not considered to give an accurate picture of consumer habits, but are merely based on income.)
- *by lifestyle* – people's general attitudes to life and the values they have play a significant influence upon the travel and tourism products and services of which they are likely to avail themselves.

Activities

- List ten tourist attractions with which you are familiar. Using your knowledge of the products and services they offer, identify the most likely market segment at which these attractions are targeted.
- Which characteristic, from geographical location, demographics and lifestyle, is most often used to segment a market? Why do you think this is the case?

An organisation wishing to gain a high share of the total market within the travel and tourism industry will try to cater for the specific requirements of as many different market segments as possible. This is possible through the use of **product differentiation.** This means a product is carefully considered in terms of how it can be adapted in different ways to meet a range of different customer needs identified through primary research methods. Different customer preferences are then incorporated into slightly different versions of the original product to cater for different market segments.

An example of this is found within the package holiday market. Tour operators have considered the varying needs of different clientele and offer a range of different packages. For example, cheap, basic accommodation close to lively nightlife may be required by the 18–30 market, and more luxurious accommodation in quieter locations required by the more mature tourist. Travel and tourism providers have explored all of the potential market needs over recent years, to offer the widest possible choice to the consumer.

Activity

Using age, gender, lifestyle and income levels as determining characteristics, identify product differentiation within the holiday market for a destination with which you are familiar. List the different holiday products that are available and state at which specific market segment the products are aimed.

'Product' as part of the marketing mix

Chapter 4 of this book ('Travel and tourism products and services') looked in detail at the main differences between products and services. At this stage, it might be useful to look back over pages 88–92 to refresh your memory on these differences.

The product life cycle

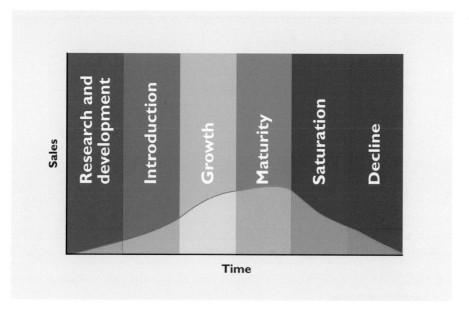

The **product life cycle** is a concept which has been adopted by general business experts to help identify the stage of development at which a particular product, service or organisation is currently operating. This information is essential in determining pricing strategies for each product, and will also help to predict patterns of demand by customers. The six stages provide clear evidence of the age and performance of specific products, which enables travel and tourism providers to make decisions regarding the manner in which such products will be promoted at any given time.

1 **Research and development** The first stage is to research customers' response to a new product or service by trials or a customer survey. It may result in the product being withdrawn from further public attention if research findings are unfavourable. This stage is usually cost-intensive as it entails primary research methods being employed to obtain direct responses from customers about new ideas.

2 **Introduction** or **Launch** The point at which the product or service is made available to the intended target audience on a wider scale.

3 **Growth** This describes a product or service that enjoys a high level of success, with new customers from within the potential market being attracted over a period of time. All businesses hope to enter this stage with newly developed products and services, as this is where high levels of profit are achieved.

4 **Maturity** Products and services are well received by the target audience but their popularity is beginning to wane. By the time

a product reaches this stage, organisations are considering future options with regard to continuation or withdrawal from the market, as sales figures will reflect the slow decrease in business activity from this stage.

5   **Saturation** This stage spells serious danger for a product and its providers, as demand falls away, and customers lose interest in a market in which products and their substitutes are too readily available.

6   **Decline** This final stage is very costly for organisations, when products and services remain within the marketplace, despite supply outweighing demand.

As you can see from the above description of the product life cycle, this is a beneficial mechanism which enables travel and tourism providers to examine the popularity of the products and services they offer in order to make forecasting decisions concerning cost-effectiveness within a selected market.

Activity

Use the product life cycle depicted in Figure 32 and mark on the diagram the position of the following travel and tourism products and services:
(a) all-inclusive package holidays
(b) space tourism
(c) the Arctic and Antarctic as holiday destinations
(d) adventure tourism
(e) a seaside resort
(f) retail travel outlets
(g) a Mediterranean cruise.

Branding is another concept widely used by businesses, including travel and tourism providers, to enhance the image of the product and service they offer within the perception of their target audience. Branding aims to create an association of the product features, packaging and price with the name of the provider. Good examples are brand images associated with some differentiated holiday packages. The 18–30 brand image, for example, of fun, non-stop activity and a party atmosphere; and the SAGA holiday brand image of holidays for the more mature traveller, of quiet locations, and more sedentary activities.

Price and special promotional features also influence the brand image created for certain products and services. For example, 'BOGOF on a week to Spain' (Buy One, Get One Free) has been associated with a specific UK tour operator through an advertising campaign. Easyjet as an organisation is associated with cut-price flight offers.

'Price' as part of the marketing mix

Common pricing policies

There are a variety of different approaches which organisations can take in determining the final price that customers are charged for the products and services they use. Many of the decisions about price depend on the type of organisation involved and how it is financed. A profit-seeking organisation will have a different approach to pricing from a publicly funded organisation which is seeking only to break even by providing a service for community benefit. The cost of providing the product or service largely determines the end price, but many other factors are also involved. The most important of these are covered later in this chapter.

Market penetration occurs when organisations choose to set an artificially low price for a newly emerging product. This is in the knowledge that customers will be unwilling to pay the full price for a product in a market where many substitutes exist amidst fierce competition. Penetration pricing is therefore associated with earning high amounts of revenue from a high sales volume, rather than through the individual value of each sale.

Market skimming, on the other hand, occurs with newly emerging products in a non-competitive market. The assumption is made that customers will be willing to pay high prices for something new that has limited availability, which they are willing to try out. Once the product has made its mark on the market and other competitors begin developing substitutes, prices are reduced to reach a wider range of the target audience.

Discount pricing is considered by those organisations who have not met sales targets either by value or volume, and whose products have not sold as well as anticipated. By offering unpopular products at discounted prices, such organisations aim to gain some revenue from the reduced price sale, rather than no revenue at all from a product.

Variable pricing, which is also known as **price discrimination**, is often a policy adopted by organisations offering differentiated products or services. One price is set for one customer type, for example a full paying adult, whilst a different price is used with a different customer type, for example reduced prices for children, students or the elderly.

Loss leader pricing is used to attract customers to buy a specific product at a bargain price, often as cheap as cost, or even below cost, in order to boost sales generally. Once customers are attracted by the bargain price, they may be tempted by other linked products and services sold at a higher profit level, thus benefiting the organisation.

Special offers or **promotional pricing** are used again to entice customers to make purchases they consider to be providing value for money. This policy encourages the concept of the customer benefiting or getting something free, via techniques such as two for the price of one, money-off coupons or free gifts.

Other factors affecting price

Organisations will consider the costs that they incur in offering their products and/or services to customers, but this is not the only consideration that has to be taken into account. A whole range of other factors needs to be considered, including:

- How the organisation is funded and whether profit generation is essential for survival. Levels of subsidies received will play a part here in determining the price.
- How much competitors are charging for similar products/services as organisations do not wish to over-price or under-charge and put themselves out of the market.
- What the customer is willing to pay. Customer expectations, especially associated with brand image, will play a role in determining the final price.
- The anticipated number of customers, as organisations have to meet targets in terms of sales volume as well as sales value.
- Seasonality – products offered in off-peak seasons may be cheaper than those offered during the high season.

Choose five different travel and tourism products and services.
For each one, select the most appropriate pricing policy, linked to
the relevant stage in the product life cycle, at which these products
stand. Identify any other factors that are likely to influence the end
price paid by the customer for each product/service.

'Place' as part of the marketing mix

The ultimate success of a business depends on its **location**, according to
real estate representatives. This is certainly the case for the majority of
travel and tourism facilities. In order to be able to draw in the required
number of users to remain cost-effective, they depend wholly on where
products and services are made available to customers. Site is therefore in
itself a significant locational factor. This can be categorised in many terms
beyond the simple factor of land availability.

As always, the **cost** of land and suitable premises will be an overriding
factor for most organisations. Certain areas are more expensive than
others depending on the **character of the locality**, crime rates, general
living costs and standards of living. The natural features of the selected
area – water resources, mountains, coastline – can play an important
role in determining the exact location of a new facility. The proximity
of the local population is also important, in providing both a potential
customer base and a **work force** for the facility. **Access and transport
links** are also vital – if the local infrastructure is poor, then additional
amenities may have to be considered in order to allow customers ease
of access to the facility.

An inbound tour operator from abroad is planning to expand and
wishes to build a new holiday complex in your country.
What factors will need to be considered in selecting the location for
this complex?
Where would you recommend the site be situated, and why?

Distribution channels

Figure 33 ▶
Common channels of
distribution

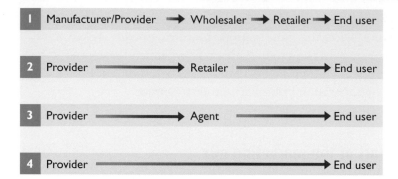

A **distribution channel** is the term used to describe how products and services are made available to customers. There are several common patterns that this might take, depending on the type of organisation and the type of product on offer. Figure 33 shows the distribution channels most commonly used by travel and tourism organisations.

In example 4 in Figure 33, the provider assumes sole responsibility for ensuring that products are made available to the consumer or customer. This is relatively common for small, privately owned enterprises in this industry and is referred to as **direct selling.** (See pp. 94–5 for more about direct selling.)

Examples 2 and 3 involve one intermediary, an agent and a **retailer**, who ensures that products reach the target audience. An agent could be an inbound tour handler, or travel agent, working for commission on the sales made on behalf of the provider, but without 'owning' the products they sell. On the other hand a retailer must firstly 'purchase' the products or services before selling them on to the customer, usually at a higher price.

Example 1 involves an additional intermediary in the form of a **wholesaler.** This is someone who buys the original product in bulk at discounted prices from the provider before selling it on at slightly higher prices to a retailer. The retailer then in turn adds on his share of profit so that the customer pays a higher price for the end product. This is relatively rare within the travel and tourism industry.

Technological advances have revolutionised distribution channels within the travel and tourism industry, with the introduction of websites and online booking facilities. Customers no longer have to leave the comfort of their own home to avail themselves of products – a click of a button brings a host of products and services directly to the home.

Activity

Using Figure 33, identify at least one travel and tourism provider known to you operating within each of the distribution channel networks illustrated. What are the advantages and disadvantages of each route over the others?

'Promotion' as part of the marketing mix

Main promotional methods

The word promotion is often wrongly used synonymously with the term advertising. **Advertising** is just one form of promotion, from a wide field of other promotional activities. However, the power of advertisements must not be underestimated, especially given the extensive range of media now used in advertising – television, radio, internet, billboard posters, leaflets, flyers, magazines and newspapers to name but a few. Generally any **publicity** materials produced by or on behalf of an organisation will act as a form of promotion, which is invaluable to an industry as diverse as travel and tourism.

Organisations will exploit publicity gained through positive **public relations** exercises. For example, press releases and published interviews could enhance the image of the organisation in the eyes of the target market.

Some products lend themselves particularly well to **direct marketing** methods. This is when existing or potential new customers are sent publicity direct from the organisation to make them aware of the products and services on offer. Travel and tourism providers often send leaflets, brochures and details of any special offers to all customers on their database.

Promotional activities, such as offering free items as part of the package (e.g. commission-free currency with a holiday booking), often stimulate interest in a product. Some organisations use **interactive media** to stimulate interest and desire, including the internet and promotional videos, emphasising the positive points of a product, facility or a service from a biased standpoint.

Activity

Collect and collate examples of promotional material issued by travel and tourism organisations in your country.

If possible, include audio or video recordings of advertisements, coverage of tourism activities or events, or press releases. Keep magazine or newspaper articles, and advertisements. Retain examples of direct marketing and mail. Explore the internet for promotional websites.

Factors contributing to effective promotional materials

There are a number of factors to consider when putting together promotional materials. These are:

- **Costs** – marketing is an expensive activity and advertisements are especially draining on an organisation's limited budget.
- Recognition of **target market segments** and appropriate media forms – ensuring that the right people see the advertisements or other promotional materials.
- **Brand image** – setting an appropriate tone and atmosphere to encourage the right people to respond.
- **Timing** – Ensuring that sufficient notice is given to enable customers to access products and services as they become available, without promoting things too far ahead so that the customer loses interest before the product is made available.

Once promotional materials are put together, the AIDA principle is often used to assess their effectiveness.

The AIDA principle

This is a way of analysing a piece of promotional material to assess how effective it is in achieving its general aim of raising awareness. AIDA is an acronym taken from the following four words:

Attention	bringing the product to the *attention* of the customer
Interest	stimulating the *interest* of the target market by showing positive brand image
Desire	provoking *desire* within the customer for the product
Action	whetting the customer's appetite sufficiently to motivate them to take *action* in acquiring the product.

Activity

Use the promotional materials you collected in the previous exercise and apply the AIDA principle.

- What techniques have the providers employed to gain attention, generate interest, stimulate desire and cause action?
- Which piece of promotional material is most effective in your opinion?

This section of the qualification will be tested by an externally set and assessed examination. The activities which follow will provide practice for the type of activities involved in the examination.

Extension Activities

1 What reasons usually prompt a privately owned travel and tourism provider to allocate a large budget to the marketing function of the organisation?

2 Consider an airline company such as Singapore Airlines. What type of market research would you expect such an organisation to undertake? Which sources of data would you suggest that they could use to produce quantitative evidence? Why might qualitative data be of more use to such an organisation?

3 What do the acronyms SWOT and PEST stand for? How do these marketing analysis tools enable organisations to achieve? How do they differ?

4 What are the 4 Ps of the marketing mix? Why are these important?

5 An adventure tourism provider targets 18–30-year-old, high-income couples, who enjoy taking risks, and who are prepared to travel over 200km to participate in outdoor activities. How has this company used the principle of market segmentation to target its customers? Where would you expect this company to advertise its products?

6 Identify three main products and three linked services of your national railway network provider. How do the products differ from the services offered?

7 Draw a sketch diagram of the product lifecycle and label each stage correctly. Identify at least one travel and tourism product or service at each stage of the cycle. How might an organisation overcome the financial difficulties associated with a product in the late maturity stage?

→ **(contd)**

Extension   Activities

8 Describe the image you associate with the Disney brand. Why do you make these associations? How might this influence your choice of product, if travelling to a destination near to a Disney facility?

9 Give one example of a travel and tourism product which would use market skimming as a pricing policy. Why does the industry offer many examples of variable pricing, in your opinion? Give examples to support your answer.

10 Why will the method of funding affect the overall end price charged to the consumer in many instances?

11 Draw a sketch diagram of the distribution channel which best portrays the way in which air transport products are made available to the customer.

12 In what way has the introduction of new technology posed a threat to the traditional role of the travel agent or inbound/outbound tour handler?

13 Produce a checklist to use in assessing how effective a piece of promotional material is in achieving its original intention.

14 Construct a Customer Profile for the end user of a Caribbean all-inclusive holiday package.

15 What do the letters AIDA stand for and how is this principle used by organisations?

Travel organisation

Learning outcomes

In this chapter you will look in detail at the range of travel providers and methods of travel, and at researching and preparing travel itineraries. By the end of this chapter you should be able to:

- explain the role of different travel providers
- identify the different types of air, water-borne and sea travel
- understand how different customer needs are met by different types of travel
- identify a range of information sources that could help you make travel plans
- identify the ancillary services offered to customers (including services relating to passport, visa, health, currency and insurance requirements)
- prepare a detailed travel itinerary
- provide a detailed breakdown of travel arrangements
- identify other types of travel information that customers may need

Some of these topics were introduced in the Core Module (Chapters 1–4 of this book). This chapter looks in more detail at the topics concerned, providing you with an opportunity to enhance and develop your knowledge and skills.

This chapter covers Optional Module 5253: Travel Organisation.

Travel providers

From your study of the Core Module (Chapters 1–4), you will have learned about different travel providers, such as tour operators, travel agencies, transport providers and ancillary service providers. Within the industry, there are many links between each provider. For example, a large tour operator such as Airtours owns its own airline and has links with travel agencies in the Going Places group. Tour operators may also have connections with hotel companies, own apartment blocks, use their own coaches for transfers and excursions, and/or even offer services such as currency exchange through its travel agencies.

Figure 34 ▶
Position of the leisure
travel industry

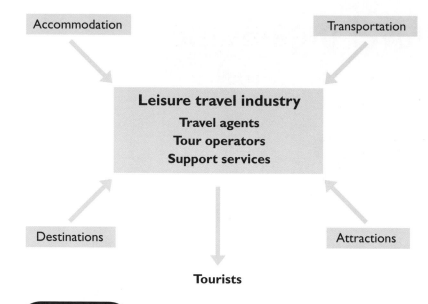

Activity

Select a major tour operator and identify its links with other
providers. You could use an organisation such as Thomson Holidays
Group or Thomas Cook/JMC as examples, or one from your own
locality.

Other providers work independently but may collaborate to provide a
travel product or service. Kuoni is a tour operator (trading under the
names Kuoni and The Travel Service) but it buys products from other
providers, such as hotel or cruise companies and airlines, to market a
'package'. This 'package' is then included in brochures issued by travel
agencies or direct to the consumer, via newspaper or internet advertising,
to appeal to particular customers. To operate the package, it may also link
with bus or ferry companies in the selected country or resort to ensure
the ancillary product or service is available when required by the tour
operator. It benefits the various providers to co-operate, as otherwise
each would have to market its products independently and might not
receive the same volume of business.

Activity

Using the advertisement below, identify the different providers collaborating to provide this package holiday:

◀ Figure 35
Holiday advertisement

8 days
from only
£499

Travel Star Holidays

Moscow & St. Petersburg
by Air

Experience the new Russia on a classic two centre holiday spending three nights in each city.

See Red Square, the Kremlin, St. Basil's Cathedral, the Hermitage Museum, Pushkin Palace, and much more!

- **Departures March to November**
- **Return scheduled flights by British Airways**
- **Six nights' half board hotel accommodation**
- **Tour Manager**

PHONE FREE for a brochure. Visit our web site: www:t-s-holidays.com
0800 32 11 14

The benefit to accommodation and transport providers is that they can have more reliable occupancy rates and offer better or cheaper rates to the operator. The operator has more control over the final product and can therefore exert more pressure to ensure the quality of provision and level of service. The benefits to consumers are that they do not have to spend time themselves building up a tour or holiday contacting all the various providers.

However, independent travellers may wish to create a more individual package by investigating and purchasing their own transport, accommodation and insurance. This means that they can select each aspect of the package to suit their tastes and requirements. However, it can take time to integrate the whole holiday successfully. Transfers from the airport to the accommodation would need to be purchased on arrival at the destination, unless the independent traveller uses an international car hire company such as Avis or Hertz who will book in advance. Many travellers in fact prefer to purchase a complete 'package' and not have the worry that something has been forgotten.

We will now move on to look at the various methods of travel.

Methods of travel

Air travel

Aircraft may be chartered for specific flights or for blocks of time, such as a specific holiday season. Many tour operators charter the aircraft (called inclusive tour by charter – ITC) on a flight series basis, contracting for the same departure time and destination each week, for example. They set very high load factors (the percentage of seats that needs to be filled before the operator starts to make a profit) in order to keep costs down. Empty seats on charter flights may be offered to individuals who are making their own arrangements, such as those who own time-share apartments or villas at a resort, in order to reach capacity. **Charter flights** may operate from a wider variety of airports than scheduled flights, and often use smaller airports or those with fewer facilities and cheaper landing fees in order to attract larger numbers of passengers from a locality. The times charter flights are given for take-off and landing have to fit into air traffic control schedules and tend to be when the airport is not at full capacity from scheduled flight demand.

Charter flights can be booked for a specific event. For example, the Supporters' Club of a large football club, such as Manchester United, may charter a flight for an overseas match, such as those for UEFA (Union of European Football Associations), and the seats sold to supporters along with tickets for the match itself. This would be arranged so that the flight arrived in good time for the match and was scheduled for departure some time after the end of the match.

The important thing to remember is that with a charter flight, whether for an event or for a package holiday, the ticket issued is not transferable or flexible. If, for any reason, the passenger misses the flight, there is no opportunity to transfer the ticket to another flight, as there may not be another flight available with spare capacity. Also, charter flights are operated for one-off or season-long bookings by the airline, and departure or arrival times may be at unsociable hours. Charter flights offer limited facilities to passengers: the luggage allowance is usually less than on a scheduled airline; seating dimensions may be more restricted; and passengers may have to pay for in-flight services such as drinks and headsets for audio. The benefits to the consumer are that ticket prices tend to be cheaper than those on scheduled flights, which brings down the total cost of the holiday package.

Scheduled flights are usually operated by the large international carriers, such as British Airways, Cathay Pacific, Qantas, American Airlines etc., and run to a timetable fixed well in advance. They usually operate from established airports both nationally and internationally. If we consider American Airlines, they operate international flights, but also operate domestic scheduled airline services within the USA. To be more economical, they operate what are known as 'hub airports'. Internal flights go to one of two or three major airports, such as Chicago O'Hare, Atlanta or Los Angeles, and passengers change there for their onward destination. To fly from Orlando, Florida, to Manchester, England, with American Airlines it would be necessary to take an internal scheduled flight to either Chicago or Atlanta, and there change for the inter-continental scheduled flight. Luggage would be checked in at Orlando for the entire journey and passengers would not need to collect their luggage until arrival in Manchester.

There is strong competition between the various scheduled airlines for routes and space at major airports, fuelled by increasing demand from both the leisure and business travel markets. Various court cases have taken place when one airline felt that another was monopolising a particular market or route.

Seats on scheduled airlines can be purchased by individuals, business organisations or tour operators. (The latter are known as inclusive tours by excursion or ITX.) They can be bought direct from the airline, via the internet or through independent travel agencies. Spare capacity on scheduled airlines is often sold by ticket discount brokers, who buy blocks of seats from an airline for more popular routes in the hope of being able to offer them to individuals at favourable rates. These brokers are often called 'bucket shops' and can provide a much cheaper alternative to the full cost fare. However, the choice of flight times, airlines and airports may be restrictive.

The benefits of using scheduled rather than chartered flights are that there is more flexibility in the number of flights to various destinations offered (because they run on a regular basis at specified times to destinations). There is some transferability in ticketing so that if you are unable to return on the flight originally booked it may be possible to change flights with minimum penalty or delay. Seating is usually less cramped, in-flight services are superior and could include free drinks and a choice of menu, video or music channel and free newspapers. Airlines operating scheduled flights also offer a wider choice of seat quality, such as First Class or Business Class service. For an international route this would ensure much more legroom (some seats have an extension that can form a small bed), more comfortable seating and better quality meal

Figure 36 ▼
A380 Airbus

arrangements. The new Airbus 380, which is currently under construction, is planned to carry 550 passengers and have facilities such as lounge and recreation areas to give passengers a more enjoyable experience and opportunity to move round the aircraft.

©Airbus – computer graphic by i3M

In response to the relatively high cost of seats on scheduled flights, there has been a development in Europe of scheduled 'no frills airlines' offering lower prices, such as Ryanair, Easyjet and Buzz. They operate scheduled flights but from airports where landing slots are cheaper and may not always be the nearest to the destination point. These airlines do not provide some of the services associated with scheduled airlines, such as free meals, but passengers can buy refreshments on the flight. Although seating dimensions are similar to those on international scheduled airlines, frequency of flights may be more restricted. The main selling point of these airlines is the low cost of the tickets. They aim to fill the planes to capacity, and the earlier you book your seat the cheaper it can be. Selling is usually direct, and may be by telephone or the internet, rather than through travel agencies, so keeping costs down as no commission is payable.

Open jaw tickets are used by tour operators and individuals when they are visiting a country and want their arrival and departure locations to be different. An open jaw ticket is a return ticket for a flight which arrives at one airport and departs from another in the same country. For example, some Cosmos tours in the USA fly into one airport, say Los Angeles, then tour round a region and depart from the final destination of the tour, say San Francisco.

An **open ticket** on the other hand is when a client, usually an individual, books a return flight or even rail journey to a destination, but leaves the date of return open within a fixed period of time. Most rail returns in the UK have a lifespan of one month. This gives greater flexibility to the client in terms of timing their journey, although the departure airport or rail terminal must be the same as the arrival destination.

Often on long-haul flights, passengers may wish to break their journey and spend a few days in a location en route. One example of this may be on a flight from Sydney to New York, where travellers may wish to break their journey in Hawaii or Los Angeles for a day or two. This is called a **stopover**. It is possible to book accommodation at the stopover location when booking the air ticket. Other passengers may need to include a stopover if they are travelling on one airline to a major airport but have to fly to their final destination with another local airline. If the flight times do not coincide, an overnight stopover may be required, but in this case it would be booked separately.

Transit passengers are those who need to change planes at a hub airport, either within the same airline or from one airline to another, particularly when there is no direct flight to their final destination. These passengers do not actually leave the airport, but follow clearly marked routes from the arrivals area to the new departure area (which may be in another terminal at a large airport). They do not usually need to go through immigration or customs until they reach their final destination. However, in the USA passengers must proceed through immigration and customs at the transit airport before proceeding to their final destination.

Water-borne travel

Ferries, including vehicle-carrying services, are means of transport between a larger land mass and outlying islands, or from one island country to other nearby countries. Examples of ferries operating between a larger land mass and outlying islands are shown in the following tables.

Ferries operating ▶
between large land
masses and outlying
islands

Larger land mass	Outlying island
Manhattan Island, New York	Staten Island (Staten Island Ferry)
Kowloon, Hong Kong	Hong Kong Island (Star Ferry)
Southampton, England	Isle of Wight
Piraeus, Greece	All Aegean islands

Ferries operating ▶
between islands and
nearby countries

Island country	Nearby country	Ports used
Italy	Greece	Brindisi to Patras
Singapore	Malaysia	Singapore to Johore Bahru
England	Norway	Newcastle to Bergen
England	Holland	Hull to Rotterdam

Ferries tend to be used for relatively short sea or lake crossings (say up to 24 hours) and run to a scheduled timetable. They may be purely passenger services (e.g. Star Ferry and Staten Island Ferry) where passengers can just walk on and off the next available ferry without reservations. Alternatively, they may also accommodate coaches, cars and lorries (e.g. England to Europe). Space must usually be booked in advance for a particular crossing time.

Services on board vary according to the length of the crossing, but usually include catering, accommodation in berths or bunks for longer routes, entertainment such as videos, films, amusement arcades and some shopping facilities for tourist products, cigarettes, alcohol and souvenirs. There may also be currency exchange facilities on services between countries, and information leaflets, guides and maps.

Activities

- Investigate the costs of ferry travel in a country of your choice for both foot passengers and vehicle transportation.
- Compare the size of ships used and type of accommodation provided along with supporting facilities.

Some ferry-type crossings class as mini-cruises, such as those from England to Spain or Norway, where the length of time on board means that accommodation is normally provided and more entertainment is available for passenger enjoyment. These crossings tend to be used to reduce the time spent driving to reach a distant destination, sometimes to reduce the overall journey time, and to provide an opportunity for a more relaxing start/end to a holiday.

The more usual interpretation of **cruises** is all-inclusive holidays of three days or more, where passengers are provided with fully equipped accommodation, stewards to service their needs in their cabins, and more luxurious surroundings. Major cruise companies produce fully detailed brochures showing dates of sailings, locations visited, the length of time spent at each destination, types of activities and services available on board and some overview of the entertainment or recreation facilities. Details are given of different cabin types, perhaps ranging from a basic two- to three-berth cabin usually on the lower decks of a ship, to luxurious staterooms on the highest deck which have verandahs and/or sitting rooms attached to the sleeping accommodation. Prices are fixed according to the level or standard of facilities, the length of the cruise and the type of accommodation. A passenger then chooses a particular cruise, which visits the locations they want, according to how much they are prepared to pay. There are usually medical facilities on board to deal with minor injuries or critical emergency situations.

Ships may vary in size and age. The newest cruise ships accommodate over 3,000 passengers, but smaller ships may be more exclusive, taking fewer passengers but offering very luxurious accommodation. The size of the ship and number of passengers on board can affect the number of optional excursions available (for additional payments) at a port of call. A larger number of passengers could add to the time taken to disembark at a resort, particularly if passengers have to be taken to the pier by tender (small boats able to moor alongside the jetty). Passengers have the choice of whether to disembark at a port of call or stay on board, and whether they follow excursions provided by the cruise line or explore more independently. However, the ship has a scheduled time of departure and all travellers must return to the ship before it leaves the port.

Cruises are not just confined to ocean journeys. There are many cruises along rivers, such as the Nile in Egypt, the Rhine in Germany and the Danube in Austria. The ships used on river cruises tend to have two or three decks only and are built more in the style of long barge or flatter-bottomed boats. This reduces the wash from the boat and so helps prevent excessive erosion of river banks.

Activity

Collect cruise brochures from a local travel agent. Using one of the brochures, collect information on the facilities on board, the size and age of the ship, and the number of passengers it can take. Compare your findings with those of a colleague in your group, or present your findings to the whole class using illustrations.

Hovercraft, like ferries, tend to be used on short sea/water crossings, largely for passenger transport. They are in fact boats which, rather than sailing through the water, ride on an aircushion over the water. This gives a smoother crossing than on traditional ships. However, hovercraft are unable to operate in adverse weather conditions as their balance on the water is affected by rough seas. The length of crossings undertaken by hovercraft tends to vary from 30 minutes to 4–5 hours.

Some of the larger hovercraft allow some access to vehicles and, as on ferries taking vehicles, bookings must be made for a scheduled time of crossing. One of the largest hovercraft is used between England and Ireland. The layout of the accommodation on a hovercraft may be more like an airline, with each passenger allocated a seat, seatbelts provided and stewards employed to provide refreshments to passengers at their seats. Some large hovercraft serving routes between countries provide entertainment on board, currency exchange and catering facilities.

Barges have traditionally been used to transport goods on inland waterways, such as rivers or canals, but are now often converted into holiday accommodation. The tourist can book a barge sleeping between two and eight passengers which is equipped with cooking and washroom facilities, sleeping accommodation (which may be in bunks), usually for a week or a weekend from a particular departure marina or boatyard. The barge has normally to be returned to its starting point at the end of the holiday. The holidaymaker choosing this form of transport wants a quieter, more relaxing form of water holiday. Some tuition is usually given by the boatyard staff on the operation of the engine and steering, information on manipulation of locks (which are mechanical devices used to raise or lower the boat from one level of water to another, such as up a hill). As barges tend to be self-catering accommodation, passengers have the choice of cooking for themselves or mooring alongside banks near small towns or villages and taking advantage of catering establishments there, such as inns or restaurants, and shops.

Surface travel

In order to explore a country or to travel to visit friends and relations, tourists use some form of surface travel, dependent on the infrastructure of the country concerned. In the more developed countries or cities there is often a variety of forms of surface travel available, with variable costs to the user.

Once the visitor arrives at the destination airport, there are various possible forms of travel available. If the visitor is with a package tour operator, then transfers to hotels are usually arranged by bus or coach for larger group sizes. Taxis are sometimes used for preferential customers or smaller groups. These transfers are usually included within the cost of the package and provide a convenient mode of transport to the destination hotel, villa or apartment. Visitors travelling independently need to arrange their own transfer from the airport. What is available depends very much on the proximity of the airport to the nearest town or city and the development of the country's public transport systems.

Buses or coaches may be available from the airport to the centres of nearby towns or cities as well as to other regional airports. For example, at Heathrow Airport in London, centrally located between the four main terminals is a bus and coach station. From there is it possible to board coaches to Oxford, London city centre, Gatwick, Luton or Stansted Airports and even cities further afield such as Bristol or Exeter. Some services require pre-booked seats, whereas others may take occasional passengers if there is sufficient unreserved accommodation. The coach services work to a timetable and most coach stations have information centres giving details of all services provided. The operators of the services could be large national organisations or smaller coach companies. Many incoming tourist guides (such as the Berlitz, Lonely Planet or AA Guides) give details of the types of transfer services available and approximate costs at the time of publication.

Some airports also run **shuttle buses** to groups of hotels in a locality – these may be provided for the benefit of airport hotel customers, or organised by a private provider and booked on arrival at the airport terminal. They may run to a schedule or on demand but can be a relatively cheap form of transport to accommodation.

Some package holidays consist of inclusive flight and car hire arrangements with the **car hire** arranged through a specified provider. Other independent or business travellers may book their own car hire through the large international organisations such as Avis or Hertz, where it is possible to book in your country of departure for the size and type of car required for collection at the arrival airport. Normally car hire involves returning the car to the same airport, but the larger hire companies may allow cars to be returned to a different departure airport. The advantages of car hire are that you can be fully independent during your holiday, taking the route you prefer and being flexible about when and where you go. There are often conditions with car hire, such as a minimum age for the driver, the need for an international licence and of course insurance against theft and damage as a minimum. The tourist may also be required to pay a deposit for the vehicle according to the duration of the hire which may or may not be returnable when handing the car back to the hire company.

Many countries provide **rail services** from the airport to the centre of the nearest city or town, or even to other locations in the destination country. The railway station is often very close to the airport, and may even be linked by automatic walkways or escalators directly to the station – very convenient when there is luggage to be carried. The trains may stop at various stations en route, or may be express trains running non-stop to the central terminals in the cities.

From London Heathrow, there is an extension of the London Underground line to the terminal buildings and a high-speed connecting train running every 15 minutes called the Heathrow Express. Seats do not have to be booked on these services, but passengers usually have to purchase a ticket before boarding. On the rail journey, there may be some services provided such as refreshments, information leaflets and maps. On the express train from Fiumincino Airport to the centre of Rome there is also a currency exchange facility.

The availability of rail travel varies from country to country, with countries like the UK, France and Japan having relatively effective rail connections to airports, but others, such as many airports in the USA, not having any rail connection whatsoever.

Rail services can also be used by travellers to visit more areas in the country once they have reached their destination resort. Using local trains has several advantages: no driving is involved, so the challenge of coping with local driving conditions and navigating is avoided. Rail travel can be a very fast and comfortable way to view the scenery and can provide opportunities to see and meet local inhabitants. Railway stations are usually in the centres of towns and cities, so the traveller can either walk or take a local taxi to the accommodation. The cost of rail travel may be higher than that of a bus or coach but is always cheaper than a taxi. However, if there are a larger number of passengers in the group (say three or more), it may be cheaper to use taxis.

Another form of transport from the airport or within a city being visited is the **taxi**, which is booked on demand at the airport, hotel or railway station. In principle these should be fast, efficient modes of transport to a destination, but much depends on the volume of traffic on the roads at the time of travel. Taxis should display whether they are available for hire, by a light or card in the window. Travellers should use licensed official taxis wherever possible. This is because a licensed taxi has a number, an identified driver who should know the best route to be taken, and a meter which logs the cost of the ride as the journey proceeds. Some other taxis may be booked for a day, or half day, after negotiating a suitable rate of charge. The driver will either take you to places you wish to visit or give you a tour of local visitor attractions within a set time scale. Taxi drivers usually know a lot about the area and its roads: official taxi cab drivers in London even have to take an examination on local knowledge and road negotiation. However, those in New York, for example, may know one small area very well, but the passenger could end up directing the driver to the final destination. Taxis are not always a cheap form of transport, but should be fairly fast and reliable.

Travel to meet specific customers' needs

Mention of **costs**, availability and reservation arrangements has already been made in the explanations of the various forms of air, water-borne and surface travel given above. The costs also depend on the number in the group, what people are prepared to pay and the level of service expected. There are various other points to consider when comparing the advantages and disadvantages of different types of travel.

Journey times for road travel may be difficult to predict, as it is not always the proximity of the airport to the city that determines the journey length, but the volume of traffic carried on the local road network. Coaches, shuttle buses, taxis and cars all use the local roads or motorways (expressways) but at particular times of the day these can become very congested, lengthening the journey time considerably. At busy times, rail journeys can be much quicker than journeys by road.

Accessibility may be an important factor in a tourist's choice of a particular type of transport. When considering how to travel tourists may consider questions such as: Is it convenient? Can my luggage be easily accommodated? Is time a consideration?

Some travellers have specific needs due to reduced mobility through disability or old age. Consideration needs to be given to the ease with which these passengers can use the service. There is now increased awareness of the need to make places and transport accessible to those with difficulties. However, coaches and buses tend to have higher steps up to the seating area, and some have quite narrow doorways that are not easily accessible for those passengers with wheelchairs or walking difficulties. Some trains may also be difficult to negotiate, but there is now increased provision for passengers who lack full mobility and assistance may be requested at some stations, or even booked prior to the journey.

Sources of information

There is a wide range of sources of information that a travel agency assistant or tourist can use to research their destination or routes. These can be produced by the service providers in the form of brochures, leaflets, flyers or advertisements in the media. If you visit your local **travel agents** you would find a wide range of brochures which are often arranged according to type of holiday. There may be a section on cruises, one arranged by country, or by type of accommodation, such as rail holidays or villas and self-catering breaks. These brochures are produced by the **tour operators** as a means of promoting their holidays, whether individual or inclusive. There may also be brochures provided by **transport providers**, such as ferry companies or airlines, again giving details of their charges, sailings or flights, destinations and facilities on board.

However, travel agencies may not be able to supply detailed timetables for surface transport, such as scheduled coach or train services. For these an individual tourist may need to contact specific providers or stations from which the services operate. The timetables produced by these operators tend to be for a specific period, i.e. summer or winter schedules, and may not always be available much in advance of the start of a particular season. If a traveller is visiting a particular country, it may be better to obtain schedules on arrival in the country and make the bookings there, rather than try to book a particular journey from abroad. Travellers may also get good up-to-date advice and guidance as to the most appropriate service and route to use when booking in the country itself.

Timetables often have symbols denoting features provided on a particular service, such as connections, catering (e.g. trolley service, buffet or restaurant on a long-distance train), provider (if more than one operator covers a particular route) and access for disabled passengers. Manuals kept within travel agencies should include some or all of the following:

- Guide to International Travel
- Official Hotel Guide
- Travel Trade Directory
- World Travel Guide and World Travel Atlas
- ABC Guide to International Travel
- ABC Summer and Winter Holiday Guides
- Agent's Hotel Gazetteer
- Apartment Gazetteer
- Hotel and Travel Index.

Tourist information centres (TICs) may be found at major resorts and coach or rail termini. These are funded by the local or national tourism authority and are valuable sources of information on the local area, though some also provide information on the country. Their opening hours vary from one location to another, and the services they provide are numerous. They usually have leaflets or promotional material produced by tourist attractions in the area, local timetables for surface transport, details of accommodation providers and local entertainments. As they have a remit to promote all the facilities in the area, they are a source of unbiased information for a traveller or tourist.

In some countries, they may be able to book seats at theatres, concerts or other forms of entertainment. They can also operate a 'book a bed ahead' (BABA) scheme, whereby a visitor travelling round a country or area can visit the TIC and reserve inspected accommodation at their next destination. The TIC takes a deposit from the customer and notifies the accommodation provider of the booking. The process saves the tourist time at the arrival destination, as it is not necessary to waste time looking for available accommodation, and also provides reassurance that the booking is with a reputable provider. Any accommodation provider used by the TIC has usually been inspected by the regional or national tourist board as to its suitability, range of facilities and cleanliness and may be graded according to standards. The English Tourism Council has a grading system for hotels, guest houses and bed and breakfast accommodation providers which aims to show some level of comparability of standards between providers (see p. 101 in Chapter 4: 'Travel and tourism products and services').

Activity

Organise a visit to a local travel agency or tourist information centre, or get each member of the class to visit a different agency, and investigate the types of information provided to potential tourists. Look at:

- the layout of the facility
- the way in which brochures are presented
- other promotional materials used by the facility (e.g. posters, leaflets)
- the range of services offered within the facility (e.g. computerised booking, currency exchange and reference manuals).

Make a presentation to the group of your findings. If others went to a different agency or centre, compare your results with theirs to identify any sources of information which may be available in one facility but not in others.

Some attractions produce their own publicity in the form of leaflets which may be available in tourist information centres, and are often distributed to local accommodation providers for display either in accommodation rooms or in the foyer. These are used to inform visitors of the attraction, its locality, opening times, facilities offered to different groups (e.g. family, senior citizen or student discounts; access for the disabled; concessions for senior citizens) and catering facilities. When these are displayed along with leaflets from many other attractions, they must be sufficiently eye-catching to appeal to a visitor, or they may be ignored or overlooked. Some local tourist boards produce packs of information to put in each guest room, so that visitors can browse through these at their leisure and pick out any of interest.

With the increase in use of information and communications technology, more information is now available through the **internet** and it is possible to find a variety of websites which provide information on national and regional tourism activities and facilities. Many of the search engines have travel sections from which you can select related sites – these may include airports, accommodation, resorts and transport providers for example. They may also relate to specific interests, such as adventure travel, activity holidays and cruises. With the increase of such information readily available to individuals, added to the ability to book a wide variety of activities online, the role of the traditional travel agency may need to change in future.

Travel agencies themselves increasingly use new technology to make bookings with increasing rapidity. **Global distribution systems (GDS)**, such as Galileo, Sabre and Worldspan, allow central reservations to be made and tickets produced virtually on demand. Viewdata systems, such as Fastrak, Istel and New Prestel, are also popular. They link a computer within an agency to a variety of providers. Fastrak is a dial-up reservations and information service which allows travel agents to access various tour operators, flights, hotels, car hire, ferries and other travel-related suppliers. It allows users to check availability, create and confirm bookings, using a variety of principals such as British Airways, Avis Rent-a-Car and various tour operators. A diagram of the system is given as Figure 38.

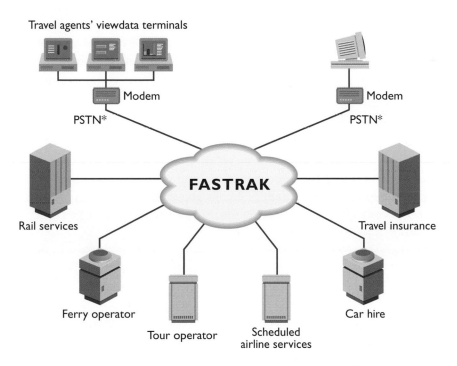

◀ Figure 37
Fastrak Reservation
System

Travel agents' viewdata terminals

Modem

Modem

PSTN*

PSTN*

FASTRAK

Rail services

Travel insurance

Ferry operator

Car hire

Tour operator

Scheduled
airline services

*PSTN: Public Switched Telephone Network

Source: *Advanced GNVQ Leisure & Tourism*, R. Youell, Longman

Other forms of electronic communication can be found at Tourist Information Centres and some main rail termini, where the customer can locate information using a **touch-screen** facility. This may provide information in a variety of languages, so the customer would first select the language to be used, then by touching the screen at appropriate points, access the information required. This may include details about accommodation, transport and local attractions. This type of technology can provide a very useful service when information centres are otherwise closed or off-duty. The customer is still helped and made to feel welcome in the country concerned.

Through the use of television, customers can also select services such as **teletext**, where travel service providers advertise flights or holidays available, often at fairly short notice. The customer then has to communicate by telephone with these businesses. The providers aim to publicise and raise awareness of their name by advertising – the offers illustrated on the screen may not always be available when the customer rings, but the business will try and offer an alternative.

When you ring travel service providers, you may be asked to select an option from a pre-recorded message. Many businesses now provide this automated facility as it is a way of efficiently directing a caller to the right department. Some travel service numbers may be a 'Freefone' number, where the provider pays for the cost of the call. This can attract more customers as they do not have to pay for the telephone call themselves.

Activity

Using one of the search engines on the internet e.g. www.yahoo.com, locate the travel section and identify the types of information provided. Select a location and print out information about types of accommodation, details about the nearest airport and who to contact for more specific tourist information (such as a Visitors' Bureau).

Ancillary travel services

One of the reasons for choosing the services of a professional travel agent to assist with organising journeys is that agents can offer advice on a wide range of products and requirements. They can provide information and services relating to legal requirements (including passports and visas), overseas currency and insurance. We will now look at each of these in turn.

Some countries have specific entry or departure requirements and wish to regulate the admission of foreigners to their country. Most travellers will need a **passport** issued by their own country in order to travel abroad. This is issued after completion of the necessary documentation and usually requires a photograph authenticated by a professional person (such as a doctor, lawyer or priest) to the government department responsible for issuing passports. These generally come in the form of booklets, with personal details and a photograph on one page, regulations controlling the use of the document on another page, and a number of blank pages on which the immigration department of the country visited can put their entry/departure stamps.

In addition to a passport, some countries also require a **visa or travel permit**. These usually need to be applied for from the consular or embassy offices of the country to be visited well in advance of the journey, as they may take some time to process. A visa application form must be submitted along with the passport to the embassy concerned, where decisions are made as to the suitability of the applicant and checks made on the authenticity of the details supplied by the applicant. A decision is then made about the application and the passport duly stamped with the necessary permit for travel often with a fixed expiry period. There is frequently a charge for the provision of a visa and payment is sent along with the application form. The cost can vary from country to country and according to the intended length of stay.

There are wide variations in **health** standards and requirements between countries. Some governments require visitors to provide evidence of certain inoculations, such as cholera, poliomyelitis, tetanus, diphtheria and yellow fever, because these may be prevalent in the country to be visited or the risks of catching the disease are high. If this evidence is not presented to immigration, the visitor may be refused entry or have to undergo vaccinations before leaving the airport. Also, if a visitor is travelling from a cooler climate to the tropical regions where mosquitos are prevalent, the national health department may advise the use of anti-malarial treatments. These usually need to be commenced some time before the journey starts in order to build up immunity. Information about vaccination requirements can be provided by the travel agent, but for medical advice you may be required to check with your local doctor or health centre as to the current regulations and requirements.

Activity

You are going to visit India and America from your own country. Investigate the entry and health requirements for each. (You should be able to find this information from various sources, such as the relevant embassy/consulate, national tourism office and travel health websites.) Write a brief analysis as to why these regulations may be in force.

Whether a traveller is hiring a car abroad or taking her own car to another country, there are certain legal **motoring requirements** in force. It is usually necessary to have an **international driving licence** showing that the person is authorised to drive vehicles in another country. This must be applied for and obtained in the home country prior to the visit. You are required to produce this licence before being allowed to drive a hire vehicle or when disembarking from a car ferry.

If you were to take your own car to another country, it may be a legal requirement in that country to carry safety devices, such as warning triangles and emergency packs in your vehicle. Therefore you need to find out about any requirements in advance of travelling. If the country you are visiting drives on the other side of the road, then it would be necessary to adapt your headlight beams to ensure they shine in the right direction while you are abroad and do not dazzle local drivers.

In addition to this, travel agency staff can also give advice as to **currency restrictions** at a particular destination. It may be a requirement that incoming visitors only bring a certain amount of their own currency into the country, or that departing visitors must declare any expenditure made in the visiting country (and keep necessary receipts) to emigration officials when they leave. This is a requirement in some of the poorer nations of the world or in countries where they welcome the importation of foreign currency but do not wish their own currency to be exported. It can also apply in a country which has a weak balance of payments but wants to encourage foreign spending internally.

While considering currency, some travel agencies provide a foreign exchange facility. However, travellers will require information about currency services and need to be aware of the various forms of currency which can be used whilst away from home. **Travellers' cheques** are often considered to be the safest form of taking currency abroad, and these can be purchased in varying values in either the home currency or in the case of major destinations (such as America or Australia) the currency of the country to be visited. In America, travellers' cheques are as acceptable as cash for payments in hotels, restaurants and shops, but in most countries the travellers' cheque has to be exchanged for local currency. The safeguards with travellers' cheques are that, providing the receipt showing the numbers of the cheques issued is kept separately from the cheques themselves, they can be replaced if lost or stolen abroad. Another benefit of travellers' cheques is that you can control your expenditure more carefully.

However, when you arrive in a country, it is usually advisable to have some **coins and notes** for immediate expenses, such as for train or taxi fares from the airport, or refreshments on arrival, particularly if local banks or currency exchange bureaux are likely to be closed. Some visitors carry all their intended spending money in the notes and coins of the area to be visited, but this has greater risk. If stolen, it cannot be replaced, which could leave the tourist with no method of payment for services or food.

Many travellers now carry **credit or debit cards** in order to pay for expenditure whilst on holiday, and they are generally acceptable in most countries. They are very portable, and relatively secure. If lost or stolen, it is possible to arrange for a 'stop' to be placed on the card to prevent it being used by anyone else. However, one danger from this is that the customer may either exceed their spending limit allowed on the card or lose track of the amount being spent on holiday. With credit or debit cards, any charges made on them must be repaid, some within a very short space of time after return, so the card-holder needs to ensure the resources are there for repayment when required.

Travellers are often advised to take a range of methods of payment, i.e. some cash for immediate necessities and travellers' cheques and credit cards for larger purchases to spread the risk. The travel agency should be able to advise on the most appropriate form of currency for particular countries. If the holiday involves visiting a variety of countries, perhaps if it is a cruise, then it may be more advantageous to take travellers' cheques in a recognised international currency (such as American dollars or pounds Sterling) in smaller denominations, so that only the amount required in a particular country is exchanged. This prevents the tourist carrying large amounts of unnecessary foreign currency, or having to pay the commission rates charged at each exchange of currency.

The final group of ancillary services included in the syllabus are those relating to **insurance**. Some travellers will disregard this, but, though it adds to the cost of a journey, it is usually considered a necessary component in tourism. Though a traveller hopes never to have to claim on the insurance, the costs and inconvenience caused should anything go wrong can be enormous. Travellers are usually recommended to insure against:

- **medical treatment** abroad should they fall ill or need hospital admission;
- **personal accident**, especially if on a holiday which involves more dangerous sports (such as skiing, paragliding or scuba diving);

- **loss of personal possessions** through theft or in transportation;
- **repatriation** (which means return to the home country) which may occur if political instability occurs and tourists are thought to be at risk, or if treatment for a medical condition necessitates an earlier or later departure than that planned, or if the tour operator or provider goes bankrupt but travellers still need to get home;
- **delays/cancellations** caused by the transport provider or the tour operator.

Travellers are advised to keep records and receipts of any payments made under any of the headings above, in order that they can complete a claim form on return which is then submitted to the insurer. After consideration of the details, the insurer may pay compensation. However, it must be remembered that in the case of lost or damaged personal possessions, it is necessary to report the theft or loss to the local police and obtain evidence from them before any compensation would be considered.

Travellers are usually recommended to carry the insurance policy with them on the holiday or at least the telephone number of the insurer so that contact can be made as soon as a problem arises. The insured person may need to confirm the insurer's willingness to pay costs, particularly for hospital treatment or repatriation, otherwise the traveller pays these costs then claims a refund on return to the home country.

Planning a travel itinerary

This section applies all the theory covered so far in this chapter to simulated situations, or, if you are working in a travel agency or for a tour operator, to real situations which could arise.

When clients visit or call an agency or operator, it is important that as much information is gathered as possible about the exact requirements of the client in order to meet their needs. It is necessary to take down personal information such as name, address and telephone number. Most agencies provide a pro forma on which to insert the appropriate information. It is also necessary to make notes of the wishes of the client, including such information as:

- chosen tour operator(s)
- destination
- dates preferred

- departure airport (particularly if the tour operator is providing a variety of departure airports)
- length of stay
- any hotel or accommodation preferences
- number of people in the party.

This initial enquiry form would act as the basis for a search of information systems by the consultant using internet or viewdata systems. An example of an initial enquiry form was given on p. 79 of Chapter 3: 'Customer care and working procedures'. It would be a useful exercise for you to complete a variety of these in order to familiarise yourself with the layout and information required. Once the availability has been checked, with the relevant costs calculated, the client then would have the opportunity to proceed with the booking or possibly have up to 36 hours to make a decision while the holiday is kept temporarily 'on hold' for them.

Activity

Mr Gerard wishes to fly from Paris to New York in three weeks' time. He would prefer a direct scheduled flight which arrives in time for a meeting in central New York at 11.00 am and wants transportation from the airport to the city centre. He wishes to return the following day in the late afternoon. His address is 24 Rue Bourbon, Paris and his telephone number is 07843 65278. He would be paying by credit card (Visa). He does not require insurance as he has an annual travel policy.

- Complete an Initial Enquiry Form in relation to this customer and check all the details carefully.
- Using the internet or paper-based sources of reference, obtain as much information as you can about available flights and costs which would be appropriate for this client.

Once you have obtained the necessary information for a client, then it would be necessary to complete a **reservation or booking form** with the final details agreed with the client.

Citalia's Italy 03 January - 31 December 2001
BOOKING FORM

BOOKING FORM TO BE RETAINED BY TRAVEL AGENT

CIT Holidays Ltd.
Marco Polo House, 3-5 Lansdowne Road, Croydon CR9 1LL
RESERVATIONS (020) 8686 5533
TAILOR MADE (020) 8688 9989
RESERVATIONS (EIRE) THE HOLIDAY SHOP 003531 679 2931
PRE-DEPARTURE ADMIN (020) 8680 5336
(Amendments, Cancellations and Queries on existing bookings)
MAIN SWITCHBOARD (other Deps) (020) 8686 0677
FAX (020) 8681 0712
PAYMENT OF ACCOUNT (020) 8686 0677 Ex 508
TICKETING (020) 8686 0677 Ex 199/236

**Visit our Website at http://www.citalia.co.uk
or E-Mail us on: Italy@citalia.co.uk**

CIT VIEWDATA

ONLINE VIEWDATA RESERVATION SERVICE
DIRECT DIAL 0345 959922
FASTRAK-CIT ISTEL-CIT #
TRAVEL AGENTS BROCHURE REQUESTS:
FASTRAK, ISTEL BP#

**OPEN MONDAY - FRIDAY 9.00 - 5.30PM
& SATURDAY 9.00 - 5.00PM**

| Booking No | | Confirmation Date | |

PASSENGER DETAILS (PLEASE COMPLETE IN BLOCK CAPITALS)

Mr/Mrs/Miss/Ms	Initial	Surname (Party leader first)	Date of Birth (if under 16)

DEPARTURE DATE		RETURN DATE		CLUB CLASS
UK Airport:		Italian Airport:		AZ ☐ BA ☐
Italian Airport:		UK Airport:		

Resort	1	2	3
Hotel/Self Catering	1	2	3
Arrival Date	1	2	3
No of Nights	1	2	3

Board Basis — Bed & Breakfast ☐ Half Board ☐ Full Board ☐ Self Catering ☐

Type of Accommodation Required
Twin ☐ Extra Bed ☐ Single ☐ Cot ☐

Facilities Reserved for which a Supplement applies:

Coach Tour or Cruise — Date of Departure
Title — Room/Cabin Type

Venice Simplon-Orient-Express
Date — From — To
Date — From — To

EUROSTAR
Date of travel — Date of Return — ☐ Return ☐ First Class
☐ Outbound Only ☐ Inbound Only ☐ Smoking ☐ Non-Smoking

EURORAIL
Date of travel
Date of travel — From: — To: Paris
From: Paris To: — 1st Class Sleeper ☐ 2nd Class Sleeper ☐

CAR HIRE/FLY DRIVE
Group — Date From — To
Collect From: — Time: — Return To: — Time:

SPECIAL REQUESTS (see Citalia Charter p.220)

SPECIAL OFFERS: Please indicate which offers you are entitled to.

IMPORTANT
It is important that this section is completed to enable you to be contacted in the event of late alterations to holiday details.
CUSTOMER'S EMERGENCY TEL. NO.

SELF DRIVE (Vehicle Details)
Make — Model
Reg. No.
Dept. Port — Arrival Port/Station
Date — Time Required
Return from — Arrival Port/Station
Date — Time Required
P&O Stena Line ☐ — Hoverspeed ☐
Eurotunnel ☐

CUSTOMER'S DECLARATION

I have read and agree, on behalf of all members of the party named hereon, to accept the Citalia Charter, (page 220) Important Information, (page 222/223) and if applicable the details of insurance (page 221). I agree that no amendment, deletion or addition will be made by myself or any member of my party to the Citalia Charter, Important Information or details of insurance. The remaining balance of payment is due 8 weeks before departure.
I am over 18 years of age

Signature — Date

Deposit of £100 per person for all bookings	£
Opera Tickets	£
Insurance premium (see page 221) (must be added to deposit)	£
Total remittance enclosed (or on credit card below)	£

INSURANCE DETAILS

All persons named on this booking form will automatically be covered by and charged for our basic holiday insurance unless you delete 'Yes' here (see page 221). The appropriate premium will be considered included in your deposits and be added to your final invoice. If you delete 'Yes' you must complete the following: MY INSURERS PROVIDING COMPARABLE OR GREATER COVER THAN CITALIA HOLIDAY INSURANCE, UNDER ALL SECTIONS ARE

YES

Citalia ITALY 2001 AGENT'S REMITTANCE SLIP Please make cheques payable to "Citalia" and send to BOOKING FORM TO BE RETAINED BY TRAVEL AGENT
Citalia Holidays Ltd. Marco Polo House, 3-5 Lansdowne Road, Croydon, CR9 1LL

AGENT'S STAMP OR CUSTOMER'S FULL ADDRESS
BOOKING FORM TO BE RETAINED BY TRAVEL AGENT

Booking Ref.	ABTA No.	Departure Date
Lead Name	Cheque No.	Value
		Switch Issue No.
Please debit No.		Expiry Date

Cardholder name(s)
Amount — Signature

▲ **Figure 38 Citalia's Italy Booking Form**

Source: Citalia's Italy brochure, 2nd edn 2001

As this forms part of the contract between the travel agency and the client, the consultant must ensure that all details are checked very carefully and the document is signed by the client. This then provides evidence of acceptance of the booking and willingness to pay the costs. Many tour operators print copies of their booking forms at the back of brochures, which can be used by travel agents or individuals who wish to make their own booking direct.

▼ Figure 39
Example of a completed booking form

PLEASE RETURN THIS FORM TOGETHER WITH PAYMENT IN LIRA TO

OPERA FESTIVAL PROMOTIONS, PIAZZA DEL TEATRO
VERONA, ITALIA 67439, TELEFONO (045)254-671897
FAX (045)254-674530

Booking Ref: 26 G.V.

FORENAME _Pierre_ SURNAME _Luclos_

ADDRESS _23 Rue de la Madeleine_

7 Arrondissement

Paris PHONE NO _23 442 3759_

HOTEL 1ST CHOICE   2ND CHOICE

Verona Palace   _Romeo and Juliet_   PACKAGE NO

_3_

DATES REQUIRED	ROOM REQUIREMENT		
JULY 17-24 2001	Tick type of room and state number of rooms required		
	DOUBLE	✓	1
	TWIN		
	TRIPLE		
	SINGLE		
NUMBER OF PEOPLE IN PARTY _2_	FAMILY ROOM		

ADDITIONAL REQUIREMENTS AND COST

COST (LIRA) _1,020,000_

METHOD OF PAYMENT _VISA_

CREDIT CARD NUMBER _6410 0069 4231 7281_

EXPIRY DATE _10/01_

SIGNATURE _P. Luclos_   DATE _9 May 2001_

Opera Festival Promotions cannot be held responsible for late cancellation due to customer illness or misfortune. IT IS STRONGLY RECOMMENDED THAT CUSTOMERS ARRANGE THEIR OWN TRAVEL INSURANCE.

Source: CIE

Figure 39 is an example of a completed booking form. You will see that it summarises all the details of the booking, with booking reference number, date of completion, client's name, address, telephone number, total cost and method of payment.

The form would be sent to organisers/tour operators so that they could then process the final confirmation of booking or invoice. There will be details about any deposit paid and the full cost on the invoice. This forms a **detailed breakdown of travel arrangements**. It may be produced in handwritten form but is more usually generated by an industry-specific computer package, which ensures that all the relevant details are included on the statement.

Activities

- Using brochures collected during your research on paper-based information sources, locate the booking forms for two tour operators. Compare the layout of the forms and space provided for the client to enter details. Read the booking conditions carefully and list those which should be made clear to a customer before a booking form is signed.
- Take a copy of one of the forms and complete it clearly using data provided by your teacher or as if you were making a booking for yourself and a friend to a particular resort.

Once the booking is accepted by the client, it would be valuable to prepare an **itinerary**. This summarises the arrangements for departure and return, and gives dates, flight times and flight numbers, and may include information as to check-in times prior to departure.

This itinerary may be the responsibility of the travel agency or provided by the tour operator, but each client should have one provided. The itinerary itself can come in various forms. The simplest one is a clear table including all the basic information, such as the completed booking form shown in Figure 39. A more detailed day-by-day itinerary may be provided for coach or touring holidays, highlighting places of interest and meal arrangements. When the client receives the tickets and documentation for the holiday, then a more detailed itinerary may be enclosed. This may be pre-printed and not include specific dates, like the example shown in Figure 40. If you were to work for a tour operator, or were devising a tour for a group of people, you may be asked to produce an itinerary in this form. This could be used for publicity in brochures or for issue to final customers.

Highlife USA
Tour 8300

DAY 1 Fly to New York. Transatlantic flight with meal and snack included. Optional in-flight movie and bar service. You will be met at the airport by your uniformed Cosmos representative and transferred to your hotel for the next three nights.

Day 2 New York City. Included sightseeing. On today's sightseeing tour see New York City's major attractions, including Broadway, the Empire State Building, Greenwich Village, bustling Chinatown, City Hall, Wall Street and Trinity Church. Tonight's optional evening outing combines a sumptuous three-course dinner with a ride up to the 86th floor of the Empire State Building.

DAY 3 New York City. Programme of optional excursions. There are so many things to do and sights to see in the 'Big Apple'. Your New York representative will offer a varied programme of optional excursions.

DAY 4 New York City – Corning Glass Factory – Niagara Falls. Depart Manhattan heading north-west to Corning to visit the famous Glass Center where craftsmen make Corningware and Steuben glass. This afternoon cross the border at the Rainbow Bridge and proceed to the Canadian side of Niagara Falls in the province of Ontario.

DAY 5 Niagara Falls. Included sightseeing. On this morning's sightseeing tour view the spectacular vistas of the massive waterfalls from above, and take a boat ride aboard the Maid of the Mist for amazing close-up views at the base of the thundering falls. Also included in the outing is a visit to the quaint village of Niagara-on-the-Lake. This afternoon your tour director will suggest optional outings including a thrilling helicopter flight over the falls and the award-winning IMAX presentation, Miracles, Myths and Magic. Tonight join our optional fun-filled musical outing all about Canada. This entertaining evening includes a delicious five-course dinner served family-style.

NOTE: The operation of the Maid of the Mist cruise is subject to favourable weather and/or river conditions. Usually favourable conditions exist from May to the end of October. When unfavourable conditions exist, a walking tour through the scenic tunnels will be substituted.

DAY 6 Niagara Falls – Lancaster. Head south following the Susquehanna River through the Appalachian Mountains and through the old Pennsylvania Dutch Country. Overnight at Lancaster, the hub of this scenic area. Your tour director suggests an optional Amish buffet dinner, coupled with a film about growing up in the Amish lifestyle.

→ (contd)

▲ Figure 40   Tour itinerary: Cosmos Highlife USA Tour 8300

Source: Cosmos Tours

DAY 7 Lancaster – Pennsylvania Dutch Country – Washington D.C. Lancaster County, home of the religious Amish and Mennonite sects, is one of Pennsylvania's most active farming communities. This morning enjoy a stop at the Amish Farm and House. A local guide explains the faith, culture, and way of life of these people, for whom tradition forbids the use of electricity or telephones in the home. Note the distinctive style of dress and the use of horse-drawn buggies in place of motor vehicles. On to Washington D.C. with a photo stop at the Capitol before reaching your hotel. This evening join the optional outing featuring dinner followed by an illumination tour of Washington's most famous memorials. Stay two nights in Washington D.C.

DAY 8 Washington D.C. Included sightseeing. Afternoon at leisure. A guided sightseeing tour of the capital includes Capitol Hill and the Lincoln Memorial. Next cross the Potomac River to Arlington Cemetery to see the graves of American heroes, including those of John F. Kennedy and his brother Robert. For the free afternoon we suggest the optional trip to Old Town Alexandria, a principal colonial port and major social and political centre during the American Revolution and a visit to Mount Vernon, George Washington's beautiful estate.

DAY 9 Washington D.C. – Fly to Orlando. A last chance to explore Washington D.C., a city 'magnificent enough to grace a great nation', in the words of its architect, Frenchman Pierre Charles L'Enfant. Perhaps visit one or two of the museums of the Smithsonian, the world's largest museum complex. Afternoon flight to Orlando.

DAYS 10 & 11 Orlando. Full programme of optional excursions. Two free days to relax and explore the many sights in the Orlando area. With so many attractions to choose from, Cosmos has put together a varied and exciting selection of optional outings. Excursions are available to Disney's huge entertainment parks, including the Magic Kingdom, the Animal Kingdom, EPCOT Center and MGM Studios. Also on the list is SeaWorld, America's biggest marine-life park featuring killer whales, trained dolphins, and its newest attraction, 'Arctic Encounter'. Other scheduled events include Wild Bill's with its western entertainment and singing waiters, exciting Universal Studios and the Kennedy Space Center. Your tour director can help with other suggestions and reservations.

DAY 12 Orlando – St. Pete Beach. Head to Florida's Gulf Coast, where the next three nights are spent at the relaxing resort city of St. Pete Beach, set on the beautiful Gulf of Mexico. Check with your tour director on evening entertainment.

DAYS 13 & 14 St. Pete Beach. Two full days to relax at this lively beach resort offering activities including tennis, golf, deep sea fishing and a variety of water sports. There is a wide selection of optional excursions to major attractions in the area, including exciting Busch Gardens. Other activities include a dolphin cruise on the Gulf of Mexico or a snorkelling trip to a nearby island.

DAY 15 St. Pete Beach. Return to the U.K. Transfer this morning to Tampa International Airport for the return flight home.

DAY 16 Home landing – in the U.K.

Clients may have specific requirements in addition to the basic holiday. You may have to provide further information based on their specific needs. For example, clients may need to know about the availability and costs of airport parking, baggage allowance, the currency in the country they are visiting and the most suitable way of taking money. They may also have questions about vaccination requirements, visas, passports and travel insurance. We looked in detail at these ancillary services earlier in this chapter on pp. 152–6. Professional travel providers need to be aware of all the information sources available, and know how these are applied to enquiries from customers.

This section of the qualification will be tested by an externally set and assessed examination. The activities which follow will provide practice for the type of activities involved in the examination.

Extension Activities

1 A tour operator has devised a package consisting of transport, accommodation and transfers, along with visits to some attractions. Explain the benefits to each of the providers through this type of collaboration.
2 Describe the differences between chartered and scheduled flight operations.
3 Give advantages and disadvantages of different forms of surface travel to a visitor to a new destination.
4 Identify and explain the types of sources of information available to travel consultants which could be used to inform a customer about a location.
5 What advice would you give a customer concerning travel insurance? Give reasons for your advice.
6 Produce a suggested itinerary for the Moscow and St Petersburg holiday advertisement shown as Figure 35 (p. 137).

7 Visitor services

Learning outcomes

In this chapter you will look at what tourist boards and tourist information centres (TICs) offer visitors and tourism providers. You will also study the range of services that can be promoted and developed for international travel and tourism. By the end of this chapter you should be able to:

- understand the role and function of national, regional and local tourist boards and tourist information centres
- identify the range of products and services tourist boards and information centres offer
- understand their marketing and promotional activities
- explain how they contribute towards quality standards in the tourism industry
- understand their contribution towards the business travel market
- understand their contribution towards the leisure travel market

This chapter covers Optional Unit 5254: Visitor Services.

Tourism is now one of the world's biggest industries with international tourism receipts approaching US$ 400 billion worldwide. Furthermore, these receipts have grown by 12 per cent per annum over the last decade and competition between countries for the tourist's dollar looks set to get even more intense. All destinations will therefore be trying to develop a consistent and high-quality tourism product to maximise their appeal and to maintain the very valuable economic impacts that tourism can bring. Leading locations receive considerable benefits from tourism and it is no surprise that established destinations like Hong Kong and Dubai (as reviewed in Chapter 2: 'Features of worldwide destinations') experience a significant contribution to their GDP (gross domestic product) from this sector. In an attempt to manage and sustain tourism growth, many countries have established specific development plans for the tourism sector. The role of visitor services will be an important component within any destination's tourism strategy.

The role and function of tourist boards and tourist information centres

The concept of National Tourism Organisations or NTOs has already been mentioned in Chapter 1: 'The travel and tourism industry' (A1 and A3 of the Core Module). The mission of such organisations is to increase the value of inbound tourism to a particular country. Frequently, the government will identify a series of objectives and the NTO will facilitate a strategy for their implementation. The **structures** through which delivery eventually takes place are usually hierarchical and the example of the UK has already been illustrated. The number of levels in such hierarchical arrangements will vary from country to country. The important point of which to be aware is that the NTO will exert control and influence from above while the local or regional tourist board will be in the front line of delivering services to the given destination's visitors. It will now be helpful to look at examples of different **scales of operation** to illustrate what precise roles and functions are actually undertaken. We will use two case studies to highlight the relevant points for this module – Dubai and Mersey Tourism.

Dubai was used as a case study to illustrate the features of worldwide destinations in Chapter 2. It is appropriate to look at this destination once again to examine more closely the role and function of the Government of Dubai Department of Tourism and Commerce Marketing (DTCM).

CASE STUDY – *Dubai*

Dubai's tourism potential was clearly identified during the 1980s. For some time, Dubai had already evolved into the Gulf region's leading port, trading centre and exhibition venue. The city therefore already had a good basic infrastructure for leisure tourism development. The Government made the strategic decision to maximise business and leisure tourism receipts and created in 1989 the Dubai Commerce and Tourism Promotion Board (DCTPB). Most countries promote tourism separately from trade and investment. However, in Dubai's case it was quite logical to combine both aspects. The worldwide promotional activities of the DCTPB, and its 1997 successor the DTCM, are widely credited with being one of the key elements in Dubai's current tourism boom. The government agency has won international awards and recognition as the leading exponent of destination

CASE STUDY: *Dubai*   *continued*

marketing in the Middle East and it has become a model to be emulated by other destinations.

The DTCM's key areas of responsibility are the international **promotion** of Dubai's tourism and commercial interests and to act as the body responsible for the planning, supervision and development of the Emirate's tourism sector. In terms of **marketing**, the DTCM undertakes the following:

- planning and implementation of international promotion/publicity activities
- international exhibition participation
- marketing visits
- presentations and road shows
- familiarisation and assisted visits
- advertising and media relations
- brochure production and distribution
- enquiry information services.

The DTCM has established a global network of overseas offices to aid its promotional strategy in various countries, and in 2001 the following locations were operational:

- DTCM in Dubai (www.dubaitourism.com)
- Philadelphia – North America (East and Central)
- Santa Monica – North America (West Coast)
- London – UK and Ireland
- Paris – France
- Frankfurt/Main – Germany
- Stockholm – Scandinavia
- Milan – Italy
- Moscow – Russian Federation, CIS and Baltic States
- Nairobi – Kenya and East Africa
- Johannesburg – South Africa
- Mumbai – India
- Hong Kong – China and Far East
- Tokyo – Japan
- Sydney – Australia and New Zealand.

The DTCM produces a wide variety of promotional materials including a variety of guides and brochures that attempt to

CASE STUDY: *Dubai*   *continued*

attract a series of niche markets by promoting specific aspects
of Dubai:

- The classic golf destination
- The watersports resort
- Tours and safaris
- The birdwatcher's paradise
- The great incentive
- Heritage and culture
- The new cruise resort
- Conference and exhibition facilities.

In this way, the DTCM actively promotes Dubai's tourism
product and brings it to the attention of a global marketplace
in an attempt to sustain and extend the number of visitors.

Depending on the location under investigation, there will be a high level
within the hierarchical structure that carries out a strategic role. For
example, within the UK the English Tourism Council (ETC) acts as the
national body for tourism in England. It has a tight remit and its function
is to focus on the national strategic framework rather than the provision
of services. It helps to raise the profile of the industry and provides strong
leadership. It currently gives emphasis to five key areas:

- research – businesses need accurate and relevant information to help
  them plan ahead;
- ensuring quality – to drive forward consistent and reliable quality
  standards throughout the industry;
- promoting best practice and innovation – to raise standards and levels
  of visitor satisfaction;
- overseeing systems for data collection and analysis – to provide
  national co-ordination of regional data to give a national overview
  and to make inter-regional comparisons;
- acting as a voice for successful sustainable tourism in England –
  encourage the industry to adopt sustainable policies and to interface
  with Government as needed.

Within the UK it is at the regional scale that the provision of tourism
services is most apparent. In Dubai the DTCM exerts total control and the
hierarchical arrangement is not readily apparent. We will now have a
look at the **operating characteristics of a local tourism body** within the
UK – Mersey Tourism.

CASE STUDY: *Mersey tourism*

Mersey Tourism is a part of a larger organisation known as The Mersey Partnership (TMP). This is essentially an alliance representing commercial companies, local authorities, government agencies, universities, media organisations and professional agencies. Its mission is to build a dynamic partnership to champion the Merseyside city region as a location in which to invest, live, work and visit. TMP is supported by the European Regional Development Fund under the Objective One programme for Merseyside and membership contributions from its partners. It also attracts sponsorship for some of its activities as well as retail income through its tourist information activities.

The Mersey Partnership **functions** as three operating divisions:

- The Mersey Partnership – the parent company
- Mersey Tourism – incorporating Tourist Information Centres and a call centre
- Mersey Conference Bureau – a focus on business tourism.

TMP is a not-for-profit company and, as indicated previously, it relies on a mix of public funding (local authority and European) and commercial income (membership fees, commission and sponsorship) for its revenues. External **channels of communication** include:

- annual report
- business plan
- website (www.makeitmerseyside.org)
- members' meetings
- consultation
- media channels.

Internal channels of communication would include things such as planning meetings, working groups and use of e-mail. All aspects of the operation are held accountable in a variety of ways, including:

- local authorities – via service level agreement
- TMP Board – has a strong monitoring function as part of its brief

CASE STUDY: *Mersey tourism*   *continued*

- government office - evaluates Objective One outputs
- members – have to deliver added value to justify membership fees.

There are many examples of the ways in which **marketing and promotion** are carried out by Mersey Tourism. Advertising is placed in specialist holiday/conference publications and occasionally national media aimed at both the public and the travel/conference trade. Mersey Tourism also produces a **range of publications** aimed at attracting visitors to Merseyside and helping visitors make the most of their visit. Three very significant examples of such publications are:

- *Liverpool & Merseyside Visitor Guide*
- *Liverpool & Merseyside Travel Trade Guide*
- *Conference Portfolio.*

Much use is also made of electronic media, with The Mersey Partnership's website (www.makeitmerseyside.org) linking in to two others (www.visitliverpool.com and www.liverpool-music-city.com). The Visit Liverpool site is the dedicated tourism section of The Mersey Partnership site.

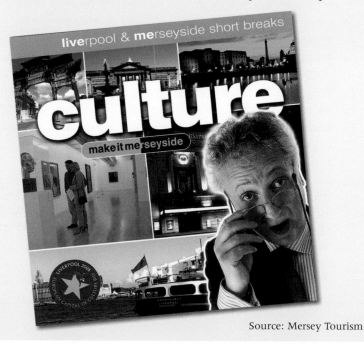

◀ Figure 41
Liverpool and
Merseyside short
breaks: Culture

Source: Mersey Tourism

Mersey Tourism is frequently involved in promotional campaigns and Figures 42 and 43 provide illustration of the 2001 short break campaign. This campaign built on the previous one and consisted of five themed short breaks to Liverpool and the Merseyside area:

- Culture
- Sport
- Nightlife
- The Beatles
- Out & About.

▲ Figure 42 Liverpool and Merseyside short breaks: Sport

Source: Mersey Tourism

Mersey Tourism's partners funded this £100,000 GBP initiative. Press releases on positive aspects of tourism are released regularly and media representatives from all over the world are invited to sample Merseyside for themselves. Visits to Merseyside are organised by Mersey Tourism often in conjunction with the British Tourist Authority (BTA), England's North Country (ENC) and the North West Tourist Board (NWTB). Mersey Tourism also participates in selected public and travel trade exhibitions in the UK, Europe and the USA, usually in conjunction with the BTA, ENC, NWTB and Mersey Tourism commercial and corporate members. Special Merseyside showcase events in selected destinations are also organised. For example, in 2001 visits were made to both Dublin and New York.

Mersey Tourism also participates in a variety of **research** activities. These usually involve commissioning research and assisting with particular studies, often in conjunction with other agencies, notably the NWTB.

Examples of research include:

- visitors to Merseyside (2000) – the major Merseyside visitor survey
- destination benchmarking
- TIC benchmarking (pilot scheme)
- hotel survey
- monitoring hotel occupancy rates
- monitoring visitor attendance at attractions on Merseyside
- survey of visitors to TICs
- production of digest of Merseyside tourism.

Mersey Tourism is seen locally as being the appropriate body to provide operational and strategic leadership to the Merseyside tourism business community. It thus acts in advisory and consultative capacities over a range of issues. It inputs on behalf of the Merseyside region into all local, regional and national tourism strategies. It also plays a central role in championing tourism quality standards and this aspect will be further examined in a later section.

Provision of products and services

Mersey Tourism runs two Liverpool **Tourist Information Centres**, on behalf of Liverpool City Council. One is at the Albert Dock and the other at a purpose-built facility that it shares with Mersey Travel in Queen Square. It also operates an **Accommodation Call Centre**. These three facilities are very much in the front line for product and service delivery. Figure 43 illustrates the range of services available. Both TICs deal with an extensive range of counter, postal and telephone enquiries, operate an accommodation booking service, sell tickets for theatres, guided tours and events, as well as National Express, Isle of Man and Irish ferry tickets. They also have on sale a wide range of local, Beatle and football **souvenirs**, publications and postcards, many of them made and printed on Merseyside. There is also a Bureau de Change facility. **Guide books and maps** are also available for tourists within the centres.

▼ Figure 43
Liverpool's Tourist
Information Centre
Services

CASE STUDY: *Mersey tourism*   *continued*

Liverpool's Tourist Information Centres

Queen Square Centre

Queen Square
Liverpool
L1 1RG

Telephone **0906 680 6886**
(call cost 25p per minute)

Opening Hours:
Mon - Sat   9am - 5.30pm
Tuesday   10am - 5.30pm
Sunday & Bank Hol   10.30am - 4.30pm

Albert Dock Centre

Albert Dock
Liverpool
L3 4AE

Telephone **0906 680 6886**
(call cost 25p per minute)

Opening Hours:
Mon - Sun   10am - 5.30pm

Email: **askme@visitliverpool.com**
Web. **www.visitliverpool.com**

mersey TOURISM
A division of
The Mersey Partnership

makeitmerseyside.org

Information

Theatre Bookings

Ferry Bookings

Accommodation

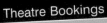

Guided Tours

Foreign Exchange

Souvenirs

Source: Mersey Tourism

CASE STUDY: *Mersey tourism*   *continued*

Information services include the promotional materials described earlier, the face-to-face service provided at the TICs and the telephone service provided by the call centre. Use is made of the MISTIC **reservation system**. Mersey Tourism recognises the importance of a destination management system and one is currently in the early stages of development. It is intended that this system will be fully integrated and customer-driven in an attempt to meet visitor needs and expectations at an initial point of contact.

Mersey Tourism is also involved with the recruitment, training and administration of 'MerseyGuides' and 'BeatleGuides'. The MerseyGuides operate an extensive programme of public walks, car, coach and minibus guided tours. They provide **guide/courier services** for the travel trade, talks and illustrated lectures as well as 'quality of life' tours on behalf of The Mersey Partnership. This latter function deals with a relocation service, emphasising the benefits of Merseyside for new employers and employees. They also conduct urban regeneration tours for students and various other groups.

Marketing and promotion

We have already seen how both the DTCM in Dubai and Mersey Tourism in Liverpool can engage in certain marketing and promotional activities. It is now appropriate to look in more detail at some further aspects of Mersey Tourism's activities. Mersey Tourism has certain principal target markets:

UK
- Consumers – 18–30s, young couples, new empty nesters (parents whose children have left home) and social greys
- Conference buyers/organisers
- Travel trade – coach and tour operators, group travel organisers and cruise agents
- Media – press, TV and film
- North West business community
- Merseyside citizens – the local population.

Overseas
- Ireland – DINKYs (dual income no kids yet) aged 20–34 and couples 50–65

CASE STUDY: *Mersey tourism* *continued*

- Spain – DINKYs 25–44
- Germany – couples 35–55
- USA East Coast (Liverpool is twinned with New York)
- selected EasyJet European destinations (EasyJet flies into/out of Liverpool) e.g. Amsterdam and Geneva
- media
- travel trade.

The drive to increase the number of domestic and overseas leisure and business visitors to Merseyside is clearly helped by Mersey Tourism's participation in various **trade exhibitions and conferences**. For example, Mersey Conference Bureau exhibited at CONFER 2001 as part of the British Association of Conference Destinations (BACD) thus raising the region's profile at this important event. Mersey Tourism similarly attends a wide variety of events including:

- World Travel Market
- British Travel Trade Fair
- CONFEX.

Certain overseas events are also attended when they take place within a targeted market area. Examples of this type of event are Dublin Holiday World (Ireland's largest travel exhibition) and Meet The Dutch Trade in Rotterdam (a BTA event).

Marketing and promotional strategies are very much informed by the use of various surveys and related research. Every five years a Merseyside **visitor survey** is undertaken to gauge the volume and value of tourism on Merseyside. The 2000 survey identified the following key statistics:

- tourism generates £604 million spending in the local economy (supporting 21,800 jobs)
- 2.4 million overnight trips were made in 2000, of which 580,000 were by overseas visitors
- 5.06 million bednights were spent in Merseyside by visitors
- staying visitors spent £236 million
- 16.8 million day visitors spent £368 million
- 600,000 visitors come to Liverpool because of The Beatles
- 1.28 million visit out of cultural interest and spend £42.2 million in the local economy

CASE STUDY: *Mersey tourism*   *continued*

- 10,400 conferences generate a spend of £33.6 million
- 58 per cent of respondents visiting Merseyside in 2000 stated that they would definitely come back in the near future.

Other sources of information allow Mersey Tourism to monitor the current state of the local destination. Hotel room occupancy rates increased in 2000 to an average of 64.8 per cent against the North West's average of only 55.3 per cent. Ongoing statistics show this to be the case throughout the period 1994–2000. Figures are also monitored for TIC usage, website 'hits', guided tours and conference enquiries. Data is thus available to inform future planning and to respond to **regional and national comparative studies**.

Quality control

Mersey Tourism promotes and champions **quality standards** in a variety of ways. All accommodation providers wishing to be a member must have The English Tourism Council Quality Assurance Scheme's graded status as a condition for membership. The ETC grades all properties and awards a rating between 1 and 5 based on a particular property's inspection findings. Hotels are awarded stars, guest accommodation receives diamonds and self-catering is also graded by the use of stars, similar to that discussed in Chapter 4 (see p. 101).

Mersey Tourism also promotes and endorses recognised **training programmes** such as 'Welcome Host' and/or nationally recognised quality standards such as the British Hospitality Association's 'Excellence Through People' scheme. Such programmes seek to develop the quality of the local tourism workforce.

Mersey Tourism seeks to recognise and reward excellence within different sectors of the local industry. Each year the Mersey Tourism Awards are presented for:
- restaurant of the year
- pub/club of the year
- performing arts venue of the year

CASE STUDY: *Mersey tourism*   *continued*

- trainee of the year
- visitor attraction of the year
- marketing plan of the year
- event of the year
- hotel of the year and small hotel of the year
- conference venue of the year
- best customer service
- tourism and the environment
- special award(s).

There are also a series of local scale **people-orientated awards** that focus on the provision of good customer service, for example Wirral Tourism Awards for Excellence. It is thus a mixture of national schemes with local initiatives through which quality and best practice is highlighted.

Destination benchmarking surveys are undertaken to update information from previous surveys on the profile behaviour and opinions of tourists in Liverpool in order to identify emerging trends. These surveys include the Regional Tourist Board's standard 'destination benchmarking' questions which are designed to measure levels of satisfaction with Liverpool. This allows comparisons to be made with other destinations. Figure 44 shows the results of the 2000 survey. Liverpool's standing as a destination can be viewed in terms of key variables such as:

- accommodation
- parking
- attractions
- places to eat and drink
- shops
- ease of finding way around
- public toilets
- cleanliness of streets
- upkeep of parks and open spaces
- choice of nightlife/entertainment
- overall impression
- safe from crime
- safe from traffic
- overall enjoyment
- likelihood to recommend.

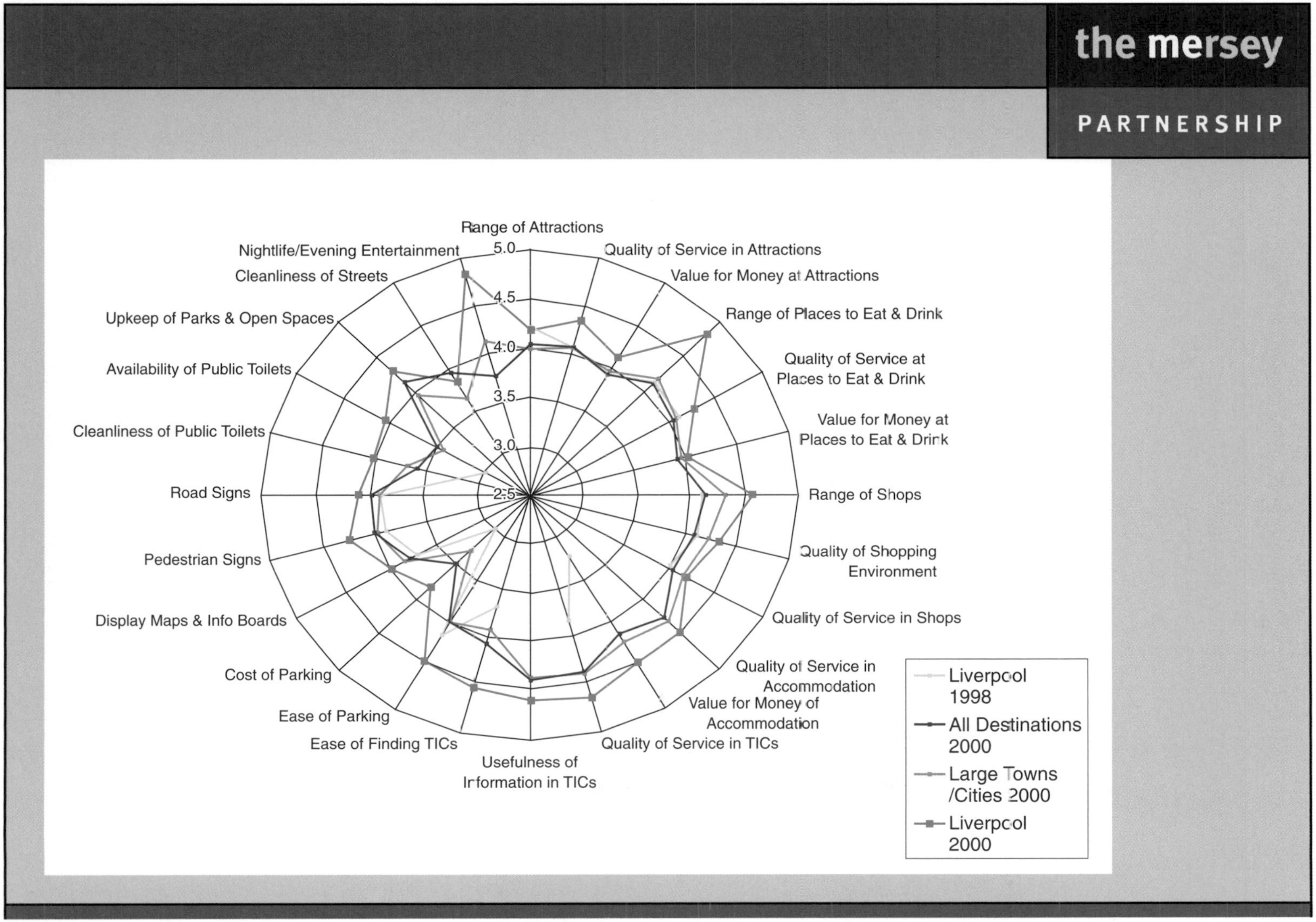

the mersey

PARTNERSHIP

Legend:
- Liverpool 1998
- All Destinations 2000
- Large Towns /Cities 2000
- Liverpool 2000

Radial axes (clockwise from top):
Range of Attractions, Quality of Service in Attractions, Value for Money at Attractions, Range of Places to Eat & Drink, Quality of Service at Places to Eat & Drink, Value for Money at Places to Eat & Drink, Range of Shops, Quality of Shopping Environment, Quality of Service in Shops, Quality of Service in Accommodation, Value for Money of Accommodation, Quality of Service in TICs, Usefulness of Information in TICs, Ease of Finding TICs, Ease of Parking, Cost of Parking, Display Maps & Info Boards, Pedestrian Signs, Road Signs, Cleanliness of Public Toilets, Availability of Public Toilets, Upkeep of Parks & Open Spaces, Cleanliness of Streets, Nightlife/Evening Entertainment

Scale values: 2.5, 3.0, 3.5, 4.0, 4.5, 5.0

▲ Figure 44 Destination benchmarking   Source: Mersey Tourism

CASE STUDY: *Mersey tourism*   *continued*

As Figure 44 shows, Liverpool performed well in comparison with other large towns and cities and with other destinations in general. It also clearly indicates certain aspects that are open to improvement.

Destination benchmarking is a very useful tool to help tourist locations improve the quality of visitor experiences that they offer.

Other places have produced innovative **quality schemes**. The Scottish Tourist Board has introduced a quality assurance scheme for visitor attractions which provides valuable information on the quality of such attractions as castles, museums, whisky distilleries, gardens, nature reserves and other such places. Three quality grades are used:

- approved – an acceptable quality standard
- commended – a good quality standard
- highly commended – a very good quality standard.

The Scottish Tourist Board has also introduced a national accessible inspection scheme that identifies, acknowledges and promotes those visitor attractions that meet the needs of visitors with disabilities.

Business travel services

Conferences, exhibitions and trade fairs are important components of the tourism economy of many international destinations. Such events can help to stimulate inward investment and the financial benefits of a thriving conference and event sector can often lead to urban regeneration and economic revitalisation. Earlier case studies of Dubai and Hong Kong have made mention of the significant contribution made by business tourism to the total tourism product. In the UK business tourism generates £12 billion into the national economy and accounts for 25 per cent of total inbound tourism. Furthermore, business tourism is growing at a faster rate than leisure tourism and, perhaps more significantly, the average conference delegate spends over twice as much as the average holiday visitor. Even during economic downturns, these forms of business tourism are more resilient than other sectors, maintaining higher levels of employment and investment.

It is to be expected that many destinations will try and maximise their **business tourism** receipts. Figure 45 provides details of the way in which Mersey Tourism has responded to the opportunities presented by a growing business tourism market through the services provided by the Mersey Conference Bureau. Merseyside is now able to supply the conference organiser with a **specialist customer service package** that gives attention to:

- help with the choice of venues appropriate to the scale of the event;
- supporting visual material (e.g. promotional leaflets/brochures to help sell the destination/venue);
- costed bids (to help secure a booking);
- range of accommodation options, if required;
- transport/transfers to make visitor/delegate movement easier;
- audio-visual and stage/set quotations arranged to meet organiser's specification;
- social and partners' programmes to ensure visitors/delegates enjoy the venue and will want to return;
- support services (e.g. business and communication facilities).

This approach to the conference business market has resulted in an increased number of bookings and the value of Merseyside business tourism generated through the Bureau is £1.4 million. One example of an important event arranged by the Bureau in 2001 was the British Council Conference held at the Liverpool Crowne Plaza Hotel from July 24–6, which attracted delegates from every corner of the world.

Conferences, exhibitions and events can all be staged in a variety of venues. It is now quite common to find several types of host venue trying to attract these types of business tourism. Examples of such providers include:

- purpose built conference centres
- hotel facilities
- sports venues
- civic buildings
- stately homes
- university and academic institution facilities.

All locations have a range of providers and it should be possible to investigate any destination in terms of the following:

- to identify and illustrate the main users and providers of conference and exhibition/event facilities;
- to describe the main locations used and indicate their relative importance;

Mersey Conference Bureau

The one stop shop can do much more than find you the ideal venue for your event. We take pride in ensuring you not only find the right place, but that your delegates truly enjoy their time on Merseyside. Don't forget there is **no cost** for our **booking services**.

ACCOMMODATION SEARCH AND BOOKING

CONFERENCE VENUES – SEARCH AND BOOKING

EVENT MANAGEMENT

BID PREPARATION

GUIDED TOURS

TRANSPORT

SUPPORTING SERVICES

TRAVEL OPTIONS

Mersey Conference Bureau
Cunard Building Pier Head Liverpool L3 1 ET
Telephone **0151 237 3935**
(From outside UK 44 151)
Fax **0151 227 2325**
E-mail **conferences@merseyside.org.uk**

makeitmerseyside.org

mersey
CONFERENCE
BUREAU
A division of
The Mersey Partnership

▲ Figure 45   Mersey Conference Bureau

Source: Mersey Tourism

- to examine in detail the facilities available in a typical venue servicing the local conference and event market;
- to describe the range of services that are available in a locality to support and maintain the attractiveness of the venues operating within the conference and event marketplace.

It is important to remember that conferences range in size from smaller meetings to international events. They are organised by particular bodies to spread information to interested parties and they are used by many different public, private and voluntary organisations. A **trade fair** is an example of an exhibition where companies show their products and services to the trade and/or the public. Other examples are more general displays of public interest revolving around a particular theme, e.g. The Ideal Homes Exhibition or the World Travel Market.

Leisure travel services

Mention has already been made about Mersey Tourism's role in the development and promotion of short break **packages** to the leisure market. It would now be helpful to revisit Figure 19 on p. 63 of Chapter 2: 'Features of worldwide destinations' to see the variety of leisure travel provision that is available within just the central area of Liverpool. Furthermore, this area offers all the ingredients for the development of successful inbound packages including:

- 32 visitor attractions
- 18 accommodation providers
- ferry terminal
- mainline rail terminus
- coach station
- local rail network access
- 2 TICs.

To support leisure visits, Mersey Tourism produces a *Travel Trade Guide* to help tour operators organise packages to the destination. Services provided to the trade include:

- brochure supplies
- itinerary planning
- Blue Badge guide bookings
- discounted admissions to attractions
- group bookings and special offers
- private tours.

Merseyside now stages a series of **events and festivals throughout the year** and Mersey Tourism helps to promote these as fully and effectively as possible. The main events in 2001 were as follows:

- January 24 – Chinese New Year
- April 5–7 – Grand National at Aintree
- June 8–11 – Mersey River Festival
- June 14–17 – Africa Oye
- June 16–17 – Hope Street Festival
- June 30 – Southport Carnival
- July 7–22 – Summer Pops
- July 27–9 – St Helens Show
- August 1–5 – Merseyside International Street Festival
- August 16–18 – Southport Flower Show
- August 20–1 – Sea Trek (Tall Ships visit)
- August 24–9 – International Beatles Week Festival
- August 27 – Radio City Party at the Pier
- August 31–September 2 – British Musical Fireworks Championships
- September 8–9 – Southport Airshow
- September 20–7 – Hamilton Quarter Jazz Festival
- November 5 – Fireworks Extravaganza
- November 16–25 – International Guitar Festival.

Mersey Tourism has established new jointly funded marketing campaigns for short breaks, festivals and events. The short break promotion has generated accommodation bookings valued in excess of £1 million and Mersey Tourism itself has directly booked some 6,000 bednights. The short break campaign won the top marketing award in the North West Tourism Awards. The visitliverpool website, with its user-friendly range of visitor information, online brochure request service and booking function receives 65,000 'hits' per month.

Merseyside now has a number of distinct product themes including:
- music – especially The Beatles and the Mathew Street Festival held in August which is the largest Beatles themed festival in the world;
- heritage – particularly maritime, architectural and industrial;
- cultural – the Tate Gallery alone attracts over 650,000 visitors;
- sport – for example, the April Grand National attracts over 100,000 racegoers;
- nightlife – world famous venues such as The Cavern and Cream;
- coast and country – from the traditional holiday resort of Southport to the peace and quiet of the Wirral Way;
- conferences – in the period 2000–1 Merseyside conferences grew by 80 per cent.

These products now form the basis for future growth in the Merseyside area. In particular, the vision for 2005 is to:

- double annual visitor spending to £1 billion;
- create 12,000 new tourism jobs;
- further develop a tourism industry that delivers a high quality, good value, visitor experience;
- establish a tourism industry that puts the customer at the centre of its activities;
- produce a responsible tourism industry that values its workforce and contributes to the economic, environmental and social well-being of Merseyside and the North West.

Mersey Tourism will work to support Liverpool's European Capital of Culture bid as well as developing new initiatives in golf tourism and eco-tourism. The opportunities for the leisure visitor coming to Merseyside continue to increase.

Assessment of this module

This module is assessed by assignment which may be devised and set by the centre or based on a specimen assignment provided by CIE, either of which is then externally marked by CIE examiners. Guidance and support can be given to candidates at the beginning of the work but only limited support during the exercise. It is important that you cover all the Assessment Objectives in this Module and your work must show clear evidence of knowledge and understanding of these.

The extension activities below will help you to focus on some of the issues which need to be developed within the assignment.

Extension   Activities

1 Undertake a thorough survey of your National Tourism Organisation to establish the policies and practices undertaken to market your country to other tourists, explaining the funding and organisational structure.
2 Describe the products and services offered by your regional tourist board or authority to promote your region and identify the possible target markets for each.
3 Invite a member from your regional tourist board into the centre to talk to students about the methods used to promote your area as a venue for conference or business activities.
4 Explain the systems of quality control used by your national tourist board or regional tourism authority as regards accommodation grading and classification and training of tourism staff.

Examination techniques

This section provides a brief summary of techniques you could develop to assist you with the externally tested examinations used for the Core Module and two of the Optional Modules. As regards preparation for the assignment required for Optional Module 5254 ('Visitor Services'), your tutor will provide you with guidance and layout suggestions for suitable presentation of your final work, which ideally should not be more than 2,000 words.

Most questions have stimulus material provided, or scenarios. It is important that you read these carefully and, using underlining or highlighting, identify the main features or key words which may be relevant for the responses. Respond by applying your knowledge to the scenarios – do not just quote textbook explanations but relate these to the scenario. The examination is testing your ability to apply your knowledge to a new situation, not your ability to remember information you have read.

The space given in the questions gives an indication of the length of response needed, as do the marks allocated to that question or sub-question. Use this information when judging the length of your response.

Remember the verb hierarchy:

Identify/State
Simple one/two word answers are required, such as the name of a provider or key term.

Describe
Use one or two sentences to give basic information. For example, to describe a package holiday you would give information such as: 'This is a holiday which includes transport, accommodation and transfers sold by a tour operator, through brochures, often issued by a travel agent.'

Explain/Give reasons

A more detailed response is required, stating often why something occurs. For example, the question: 'Explain customer service, or what do you understand by customer service?' This would require a response such as 'Customer service is the manner in which an organisation behaves towards its customers, whether internal or external. This includes the procedures for handling complaints, the attitude and behaviour of staff to customers whether face-to-face, on the telephone or in writing. If customer service is good then the organisation will benefit from repeat business.'

Analyse/Compare

This needs a detailed response and candidates need to show they can compare data. An example could be: 'What environmental impacts would a new development have on this area?' This needs at least one positive and one negative impact explained and some expansion of the answer to give the benefits or drawbacks to a locality – e.g. conservation/preservation as plus point; litter, pollution, noise as minus points. If more points are given then higher marks can be achieved.

Evaluate

This needs a higher level response showing breadth of knowledge and your ability to apply this knowledge to a scenario. You need to include facts but also some element of reasoning into your response, or justification for your comments/suggestions. These questions are often marked on a 'level of response' basis by examiners, which means that the more depth and understanding shown by the candidate, the higher the marks awarded.

Useful websites

The following is a list of websites that you may find useful, selected from the large number of sites relevant to the travel and tourism industry.

Air Transport Association: www.airlines.org

Association of British Travel Agents (ABTA): www.abta.com

Excite Maps: www.excite.com

Fodor's Travel Online: www.fodors.com
Information for travellers based on Fodor's travel publications, including destination guides.

InfoHub, Inc. (special interest holidays): www.biztravel.com

International Air Transport Association (IATA): www.iata.org

International Civil Aviation Organisation (ICAO): www.icao.int

International Society of Travel Medicine: www.istm.org

International Tourist Bureaus: www.armchair.com/bureau/inttb/html

International Tourist Offices: www.tvlon.com/resources/

Lonely Planet Online: www.lonelyplanet.com
Information for travellers based on Lonely Planet publications, including destination guides.

MapQuest!: www.mapquest.com

Round-the-World Travel Guide – Airlines: www.travel-library.com/rtw/html/rtwairlines.html

Travel Health Online: www.tripprep.com

Travel and Leisure: www.travelandleisure.com
An open website including up-to-date travel articles.

Weather Channel: www.weather.com/homepage.html

World city maps: www.lib.utexas.edu/maps/maps_sites/cities_sites.html

World Health Organization: www.who.int

World time locations: www.worldtimeserver.com

World time zone converter: www.timezoneconverter.com

World time zones: www.worldtimezone.com

World Tourism Organization: www.world-tourism.org

Worldwide Airport and City Code Database: www.airportcitycodes.com

Glossary of terms

accommodation – a general term used to denote any form of facility that acts as a living area and provides facilities for sleeping, e.g. hotels, hostels, caravans

amalgam destination – an area that offers a combination of attractions, e.g. natural landscape, accommodation facilities and built attractions

assets – the funds and property of an organisation, or the facilities in a region such as landscape, heritage etc.

Association of British Travel Agents (ABTA) – a UK trade association for tour operators and travel agents

attacking strategy – where an organisation aims its marketing to fight competition in that market segment, often with offers and promotions

attitudes – the way an employee behaves, thinks and feels about the tasks being performed

attraction – something a tourist wants to see or visit; attractions can be natural, e.g. Table Mountain in Cape Town, or built, e.g. Disney World

balance of payments – statement showing a country's income earned from foreign countries compared with the amount it spends in overseas markets

business – for the purpose of trade or commerce rather than for leisure or personal reasons

catering – providing refreshment, namely food and/or drink

classification – a way of categorising something based upon common characteristics

climate – the general condition of an area in terms of temperature, rainfall, humidity, etc.

commercialisation – making a service or product generally public, through advertising and other forms of promotion

component – a part or section which makes up a whole

concentrated marketing – marketing to a narrow market segment to develop the ideal offer and marketing mix

conservation – protecting from damage, and managing buildings, artefacts and landscape in such a way that they can be enjoyed by future generations

continent – the six major land masses of the earth

cooler humid – climate denoted by rain and severe weathers

cost of living – general economic determinant denoting everyday expenses in terms of food, housing costs, etc.

cultural – the characteristics and behaviour shared by a nation or group

day visitor – someone who visits an area outside their normal place of residence, but who returns home to sleep rather than staying overnight

defensive strategy – where an organisation aims its marketing to retain its share of the market to defend its position in that market

demographic information – data relating to human population, e.g. age, sex, family size, employment

deregulate – the gradual removal of government controls over transport competition, which has led to special offers and new fares

destination – the end point of a journey, irrespective of its purpose

differentiated marketing – marketing to several market segments, developing an effective offer and marketing mix for each

diversification – the practice of broadening a range of products or services which a business depends on, or of introducing products into new markets

dry – climate denoted by semi-arid and desert-like conditions

economic – the financial aspects of an issue

economies of scale – the continuing of two or more tour operators, for example, which allows them to reduce their total costs by negotiating better rates from their suppliers because of their increased purchasing power

ecotourism – tourism stimulated by the ecology (nature, culture, heritage) of an area

environmental – affecting the physical surroundings and living areas

external customer – client group outside a business organisation

flow diagram – a chart used to show a model of how information can flow from one system to another

global position – literally denoting location upon the world globe

Greenwich Mean Time (GMT) – the time at the zero meridian of longitude, from which all others are calculated

gross domestic product (GDP) – the revenue earned within a country from the sales of goods and services provided by that country

host community – local residents in an area of tourism

incentive – prize or award offered to encourage business or motivate staff

incentive travel – specialist section of the industry that handles incentive travel trips

information services – the provision of details, data and information for public use

infrastructure – the roads, bridges, railway lines and stations, telecommunications, power supplies, gas mains etc. of a country or region

integration – the growing trend for providers of travel services to integrate their products, such as a tour operator with a travel agent and/or a charter airline

internal customer – people within other departments or sister organisations requiring the services offered

international – existing, involving or carried on between two or more nations

International Air Transport Association (IATA) – organisation controlling policies relating to competitive airline organisations

itinerary – schedule or plan of activities

knowledge – factual understanding of systems, procedures and specific job roles

landmass – major continents such as Europe, Africa, Asia discernible from the air

latitude – imaginary horizontal lines used to divide the earth for navigation purposes

leisure – free time or time at one's disposal

local authority – bodies responsible for local government decisions, such as country, borough, district or parish councils

longitude – divisions of the globe passing vertically from the zero meridian, which runs through Greenwich in London UK

mail-merge – using a database to individualise a standard letter through the means of Information and Communications Technology

major city – one that attracts a large number of tourists as an amalgam destination

market research – method of finding out the needs and wants of consumers, using primary and secondary research methods

marketing mix – a set of controllable variables and their levels that the firm uses to influence the target market

marketing strategy – a set of objectives, policies and rules that guides the firm's marketing effort – its level, mix and allocation – partly independently and partly in response to changing environmental and competitive conditions

maximise – achieve the best benefit from, make the most of

media – means by which information is passed on to the public

multi-dimensional – looking at a wide range of characteristics a locality may offer, whereby more than one aspect of a locality is available to appeal to a wider audience

multiplier effect – the principle that expenditure on one economic activity, such as tourism, has an effect on the turnover of other businesses in the same location

national – generally of, or belonging to, one nation; nationwide

negotiation – means of coming to a common agreement, through discussion and compromise

objectives – specific aims and purpose

ocean – large sea

other native language speaker – someone whose main language is different from that generally spoken in an area

package holiday – the pre-arranged combination of overnight accommodation, transport and other tourist services for a period of more than 24 hours

Polar – of or relating to the poles

political factors – influences of governments on development, security and freedom of movement to encourage regional developments

pollution – the spoiling of the environment by the impact of harmful substances such as effluent and noise

preservation – maintaining items such as nature, buildings and artefacts in their present form

primary research – research undertaken first hand; field research

principal – an individual or organisation responsible for organising or providing some sort of product, service or facility

private sector – funding for the business is provided from private funds of individuals or shareholders with the aim of making a profit for the individual or shareholder

promotion – the marketing and advertising of a product or service

provider – individual or organisation that lays on specific products, services and facilities for the use of others

public sector – where the provision of funding for an attraction/region comes from government or local authority finances collected through rates and taxes

purpose of visit – the reason motivating the visit

qualities – personal characteristics necessary for employment

rate of inflation – a percentage increase in the cost of living

regional – an area of land having defined boundaries

resort – a city, town, village or other development visited by tourists for a specific purpose

retailer – a distributor that sells products or services directly to consumers

sampling – methods of collecting information from a selected group in order to make predictions about the behaviour and habits of the population in general

sea – a large body of salt water

seasonal – affected by the changing seasons of the year, relating specifically to one or more of the seasons

secondary research – the use of others' data; desk research

secondary spending – money spent by visitors on items other than admission to a facility or attraction, e.g. on food or on souvenirs

self-catering accommodation – any type of accommodation that allows and expects guests to arrange their own meals

serviced accommodation – any accommodation provided by an organisation that offers a range of additional services beyond sleeping facilities

services – any activity or benefit offered by one party to another

skills – specific knowledge, understanding and talents that prepare people for employment

social – relating to a community

sustainable tourism – meeting the needs of the present without compromising the ability of future generations to meet their own needs

tour operator – organisation that puts together inclusive holidays to sell to the public

tourism policy – official regulations controlling tourist activity within a given region

tourist information centre (TIC) or tourist information office – public-sector information service located in town centres and points of entry to areas, such as railway stations, offering advice and information, often able to make accommodation reservations

tours – a trip visiting a number of places

transport – a means of getting from one place to another

transport hub – main centre for a specific means of transport, e.g. airport, railway terminus

transport links – network linking tourist attractions and destinations through a variety of means of transport

travel agency – a shop or office providing services related to the provision of travel, transport and holiday packages

travel centre –a shop or office that provides information and booking services for transport

travel services – the provision of information, advice, and sales of transport, holidays etc.

triangular relationship – involves the host community, environment and tourist or tourism provider working together or co-operating to sustain tourism

tropical humid – climate denoted by rain and moderate/mild winters

undifferentiated marketing – marketing aimed at the largest part of the market with one offer and marketing mix trying to attract as many customers as possible

Universal Time Co-ordinate (UTC) – zero meridian of longitude, also known as GMT

visiting friends and relatives (VFR) – travel or tourism activities involving the visiting of family or friends who reside outside your own place of residence

visitor attractions – see attraction

voluntary sector – funding and support is provided by volunteers with no direct aim to making a profit

warmer humid – climate denoted by rain with mild winters

wholesaler – distributor who passes on products or services to retailers

world time zones – areas of the globe affected by meridians of longitude

Acknowledgements

We are grateful to the following for permission to reproduce photographs:

NASA p31; Hotel Elizabeth Rockingham p72; Wheelchair Travel, Guildford p76; Boeing p108; Airbus p140

We would like to thank the following for permission to use their material in either the original or adapted form:

Air Portugal, Citalia Holidays Ltd, Club Med UK, Columbus Publishing, Cosmos Tours, Dominica Tourist Board, English Tourism Council, Government of Dubai Department of Tourism and Commerce Marketing, Government of India Tourist Office, Grenada Board of Tourism, Holiday Autos, Hong Kong Tourism Board, IATA, Japan National Tourist Organisation, Jebel Ali Hotel, Lunn Poly, Marriott Hotels, Pearson Education, Seafrance, Six Continents Hotels, Sovereign Holidays, The Mersey Partnership, Tunisia National Tourist Office, World Tourism Organization.

Figures 23a, 23b and 39 are reproduced by permission of the University of Cambridge Local Examinations Syndicate.

Every effort has been made to reach copyright holders. The publishers would be pleased to hear from anyone whose rights they have unwittingly infringed.

The publisher has used its best endeavour to ensure that the URLs for external websites referred to in this book are correct and active at the time of going to press. However, the publisher has no responsibility for the websites and can make no guarantee that a site will remain live or that the content is or will remain appropriate.

Index

accessibility
  of airports, 104–105
  of Dubai, 41–42
  and transport, 28, 129, 147
  for visitors with disabilities, 178
accommodation
  advertising for, 9
  all-inclusive type, 9
  bed and breakfast, 9, 101, 102
  bookings of, 14
  on cruise ships, 92, 143
  full board type, 9
  grading systems for, 101, 149, 175
  half board type, 9
  occupancy rates of, 103, 171, 175
  principals for, 9
  products of, 90
  profit from, 102
  self-catering type, 9, 100–101, 144
  serviced, 9, 100
  services for, 90
  for stopovers, 141
  and Tourist Information Centres, 14
Accommodation Call Centre, Liverpool, 171, 173
Adriatic Sea, 33
adventure holidays, 28
advertising
  media for, 131
  in Mersey Tourism, 169
  on teletext, 152
  by travel agents, 6
Africa, 33, 35, 39, 116
age groupings, 55, 70, 71–72
AIDA principle, 132
Air Transport Action Group, 112
air travel
  chartered flights, 8, 109, 138
  deregulation of, 111
  domestic services in, 106
  growth in, 109–110
  regulation of, 110–111

  scheduled flights, 8, 107–108, 138–140
  ticket types in, 141
  in USA, 34–35, 107
Airbus 380, 140
airlines
  catering by, 11
  competition between, 139
  and governments, 108
  improved technology of, 27
  national type, 108
  'no frills' type, 140
  pollution from, 22
  as principals, 8, 11
  and ticket prices, 140–141
  in USA, 107
airports
  accessibility of, 104–105
  hub type, 100, 106, 107, 139, 141
  on islands, 28
  regional type, 100
  traffic through, 34–35, 38
  in USA, 107
Alps, 40, 53–55
amalgam destinations, 40–41, 45, 61
America, North, 33
  see also Canada; USA
America, South, 33, 35
Amish communities, 161, 162
ancillary services, 89, 92, 152–156
Antarctic Circle, 37
Antarctica, 33
anti-malarial treatments, 153
Arabian Gulf, 40, 41
Arctic Circle, 37, 38
Asia, 33, 35
Association of Independent Tour Operators, 95
Atlantic Ocean, 33
audio guides, 15
Australasia, 33
Avis car hire, 137, 145–146
awards for tourism, 175–176, 182

balance of payments, 18, 19, 154
Balearic Islands, 55
Baltic Sea, 33
Bangkok, 39
Barbary coast, 56
Bardo Museum, 56
barge holidays, 144
Beatles tourism, 171, 174, 182
BeatleGuides, 173
bed and breakfast, 9, 101, 102
benchmarking of destinations, 171, 176,
        177, 178
Berbers, 56
Black Sea, 33
Blue Train, 115
BOGOF brand image, 126–127
book a bed ahead scheme, 149
booking
    of accommodation, 14
    book a bed ahead scheme, 149
    confimation of, 81, 159–160
    information for, 77–79
    and mobility problems, 148
    online, 73, 74, 150
    records of, 77–79
    by travel agents, 6
booking forms, 80, 157, 158, 159
branding, 126–127, 128, 132
British Airports Authority, 107–108
British Association of Conference Destinations,
    174
British Council Conference, 179
British Heritage Tours, 95
British Hospitality Association, 'Excellence
        Through People' scheme, 175
British Incoming Tour Operators Association, 95
British Summer Time, 37
British Tourist Authority, 13
    and domestic tourism, 4
    and inbound tourism, 4
    and international tourism, 4, 29
    and Mersey Tourism, 170
    and national tourism bodies, 14
    and outbound tourism, 5
    and regional tourism bodies, 14
    and spending by tourists, 17
British Travel Trade Fair, 174
brochures
    booking forms in, 159
    for Club Med, 53, 54
    for Dubai, 166–167
    from National Tourism Organisations, 23
    from tour operators, 7, 39, 92, 131, 148

    in Tourist Information Centres, 14
    for trade fairs, 93
    from transport providers, 131, 148
    from travel agencies, 6, 148
bucket shops, 139
Bulla Regia, 57, 58
buses, 104, 106, 145
business tourism, 12
    car hire for, 9
    in Dubai, 42, 45–48, 178
    facilities for, 90, 98, 103
    in Hong Kong, 178
    host venues for, 179
    and Mersey Tourism, 179–181
    statistics of, 4, 5
    travel agencies for, 5, 6–7
business travel services, 178–181
business travel specialists, 98

Cadbury World, UK, 11
Cambodia, 27
Canada, 116
cancellations, 156
Cancer, Tropic of, 37
Capricorn, Tropic of, 37
car hire, 9, 137, 145–146
car travellers, facilities for, 116
Caribbean, 28
Caribbean Sea, 33
Carrier Specific Display, 82
cars' headlight beams, 154
Carthage, 56, 58
catering facilities, 11, 90
Center Parcs holiday villages, 101
central reservations systems, 7, 82
chartered flights, 8, 109, 138
Chemtou, 57
Chenini, 57
Chicago O'Hare Airport, 104, 139
China, 27, 61, 84
    see also Hong Kong
Ciampino airport, 105
Citalia's Italy booking form, 158
cities as transport hubs, 34–35
climate, 38–40, 42, 53
Club Med holiday brochure, 53, 54
coach services, 104, 106, 145
Comfort Inns, 9
Commerce and Tourism Promotion Board,
        Dubai, 165
commission
    on currency exchange rates, 92–93
    fee for, 97

as incentive, 97
override type, 98
for travel agent, 130
communication, 69, 70–72, 73, 168–169
electronic, 151–152
comparative studies in tourism, 175
competition, 65–66, 128, 139, 164
competitive advantage, 119
complaints, 67–69
computer reservation systems, 6, 73, 81
computerised information databases, 82
conferences, 174, 175, 178, 182
confirmation of booking, 81, 159–160
Congo, 27
conservation, 11, 22, 28, 53
consumer needs, 28
see also customers
consumer protection, 24, 96
Convention and Exhibition Centre, Hong Kong,
61
Cook, Thomas, 7, 105
Corning Museum of Glass, USA, 11, 161
Cosmos, 95, 141, 161–162
Costa Rica, 27
courier services, 173
credit cards, 155
crime, 16
cruises
accommodation on, 92, 143
and Hong Kong, 59
infrastructure for, 100
on oceans/rivers, 143
routes for, 114
Cuba, 27
cultural differences, 70, 72
cultural heritage, 11, 16, 42–43, 182
cultural impacts, 15–17
currency exchange facilities, 146, 154
currency exchange rates, 85, 92–93
currency requirements, 155
currency restrictions, 154
customer base, 65, 119
customer care
aims of, 64
handling enquiries, 74–75
policies for, 64–69
profit from, 65, 119
and satisfaction, 120
support for, 7
customer complaints, 67–69
customers, 71
anticipated numbers of, 128
assistance for, 75

databases of, 121, 131
external/internal type, 66–67
needs of, 75, 156–157, 160, 163
safety of, 76
special needs of, 69, 70, 178
and tour operators, 137
of Tourist Information Centres, 75, 171, 175
travel agencies, 159
word of mouth recommendations by, 66
see also visitor numbers; visitor surveys

Dar Annabi, 56
Dar Ben Abdullah, 56
data collection, 121, 167
day trippers, 12, 58
Daylight Saving Time, 37
debit cards, 155
delays, 156
demographic factors in marketing, 123
demonstration effect, 16
Department of Tourism and Commerce
Marketing, Dubai, 43, 48, 165, 166–167
deposits, 6, 77–79, 78
deregulation of air travel, 111
destinations
for age groups, 55
amalgam type of, 40–41, 45, 61
benchmarking of, 171, 176, 177, 178
city-break type, 59
guides for, 82
information on, 50
long-haul type, 28, 59, 141
visitor attractions as, 99
destinations management system, 173
Detroit, 39
developing countries, 11–12, 21, 27, 154
development finance, 24
Dido, 58
direct marketing, 131
direct selling, 7, 94, 130
directories, 82
disabled visitors, 148, 178
discount pricing, 128
Disney theme parks, 11
disposable incomes, 28, 29
distribution channels, 130
Dominica, 51, 52, 53
Dougga, 56, 57, 58
Dubai, 164
accessibility of, 41–42
as amalgam destination, 40–41, 45
brochures for, 166–167
business tourism in, 42, 45–48, 178

climate of, 42
Commerce and Tourism Promotion Board, 165
cultural heritage of, 42–43
Department of Tourism and Commerce
        Marketing, 43, 48, 165, 166–167
government of, 43, 165–166
Gross Domestic Product of, 40
hotels in, 48–50
infrastructure of, 43, 48
leisure tourism in, 42
location of, 41
map of, 46–47
positive effects of tourism, 16
promotional material for, 166–167
sports facilities in, 44–45
UK tourists for, 44
visitor attractions of, 42
visitor survey of, 41
Dubai Duty Free, 43
Dubai International Airport, 41
Dublin Holiday World, 174

Earth, 31, 32
economic impacts of tourism, 17–21, 28, 164
economies of operation, 102
economies of scale, 94
economy
   local, 17, 18, 20
   national, 7
eco-tourism, 52–53, 183
Ecuador, 27
electronic communication, 151–152
electronic media, 169
employment, 17, 20, 21
   see also staff
England's North Country, 170
English Channel, 33
English Tourism Council, 149, 167
   Quality Assurance Scheme, 175
enquiries, handling of, 74–75
environmental impacts of tourism, 22
environmental protection, 53
Equator, 37, 38
European Capital of Culture bid, 183
European Union Directives, 96
Evans Tours, 95
'Excellence Through People' scheme, British
        Hospitality Association, 175
exchange rates, 85, 92–93
exhibitions, 174, 178

facilities
   for business tourists, 90, 98, 103
   for car travellers, 116
   for leisure tourists, 103
Fairview Inns, 102
Fastrak, 151
ferries, 141–143
   infrastructure for, 100
   operators of, 8, 11
   routes for, 112, 113–114
festivals, 181–182
France, 29, 55
free offers, 131
Freefone numbers, 152
Friends of the Earth, 22
funding priorities, 21

generators of tourism, 28
Ghana, 27
global distribution systems, 151
globalisation, 31
Going Places group, 135
golf, 44, 183
governments
   and airlines, 108
   of Dubai, 43, 165–166
   and infrastructure, 23
   and promotion, 23–25
   statistics from, 121
   and tourism, 22, 23–25
   and visitor attractions, 24
grading systems for accommodation, 101, 149,
        175
Grand National, 182
Greenwich Mean Time, 37
Greenwich Meridian, 36–37
Grenadines, 28
Gross Domestic Product, 18, 40, 164
Guadeloupe, 52
guesthouses, 101
guide books, 15, 82, 104–105, 171
guide services, 15, 92, 145, 173, 175

Hannibal, 56
Hatta Fort Hotel, 50
health and fitness, 28, 89
health and safety, 24
health centres, 153
health standards, 153
Hertz car hire, 137, 145–146
Highlife Breaks, 95

holiday fairs, 93
Holiday Inn, 9, 102
holiday parks, 101
holiday resorts, 182
holiday villages, 101
Hong Kong
    business tourism in, 178
    Convention and Exhibition Centre, 61
    and cruises, 59
    as holiday destination, 59–61, 164
    map of, 60
    recreation in, 61
    special events in, 59
    tours of, 59, 61
    visitor attractions of, 61
horse racing, 44
host community, 15–17, 21
host venues, 179
hotel chains, 99, 102
hotel surveys, 171
hotels, 48–50, 101
hovercraft, 144
hub airports, 100, 106, 107, 139, 141
humidity, 39

inclusive tours by excursion, 139
India, 116
Indian Ocean, 33
inflation, 21
information
    for bookings, 77–79
    for customers' needs, 75, 156–157, 160, 163
    on destinations, 50
    on internet, 25
    sources of, 82, 148–152, 163
    and staff, 50, 52
information communication technology, 27,
    73, 150
information packs, 150
information services, 173
infrastructure
    for cruises, 100
    of Dubai, 43, 48
    funding for, 21
    and governments, 23
    for private developers, 99–100
    for road transport, 116
    for tourism, 16, 98, 99
initial enquiry form, 79, 157
inoculations, 153
insurance cover, 97, 155–156
integrated rapid transit systems, 104
integration, 94

interactive media, 131
International Air Transport Associations,
    110–111
International Date Line, 37
international driving licence, 154
international tourism, 4, 29
internet, 25, 95, 150
    see also websites
interpersonal skills, 69–70
interviews for promotion, 131
interviews for research, 121
investment, 102
Iran, 27
Irish Sea, 33
island airports, 28
Israel, 27
Italy, 29, 55
itineraries, 83–84, 156–160, 161–162

Jamaica, 28
Japan, 29, 116
Jebel Ali Hotel and Golf Resort, 48–50
El Jem, 57, 58
job creation, 17, 20
job satisfaction, 66
joint-venture operations, 102
journey times, 147

Kairouan, 57, 58
Kenya, 39
Khor Dubai Wildlife Sanctuary, 42

land costs, 129
language difficulties, 16, 17, 70, 72
languages
    in guide books, 15
    for touch-screen facilities, 151–152
Last Seat Availability, 82
latitude, 37–38
leaflets, 14, 131, 150
leakage from local economy, 20
Lebanon, 27
leisure facilities, 16, 90
leisure tourism, 4, 5, 12, 42, 103
leisure travel services, 181–183
Leonardo da Vinci airport, 105
Lesser Antilles, 52
lifestyle, 123
listening skills, 69, 70–71
Liverpool
    European Capital of Culture bid, 183
    map of centre, 63
Liverpool & Merseyside Travel Trade Guide, 169, 181

Liverpool & Merseyside Visitor Guide, 169
Liverpool City Council, 171
Liverpool Crowne Plaza Hotel, 179
local economy, 17, 18, 20
local facilities, 16
local people, 21, 22
  see also host community
London taxis, 147
London Underground, 146
long-haul destinations, 28, 59, 141
longitude, 37
Los Angeles, 139
loss leaders, 128
loss of personal possessions, 156
luggage, 147

Al Maha, 42
Maktar, 56, 57
manuals, 82, 149
market penetration, 127
market research, 7, 11, 23, 120–121
market segmentation, 123–124, 132
market skimming, 127
marketing, 93
  costs of, 132
  direct type, 131
  and Dubai DTCM, 166
  and National Tourism Organisation, 13
  and niche marketing, 167
  of package, 136
  by principals, 10
  and profit, 12
  and promotion, 119–123, 131–132, 169–171,
    173–174
  targets for, 123–124, 132, 173–174
marketing analysis tools, 121–122
marketing mix
  4 Ps, 122
  and place, 129–130
  and price, 127–129
  products in, 124–127
  and promotion, 131–132
Marriott Hotels, 9, 102
Martinique, 52
Mathew Street Festival, 182
media, 28, 131, 169
medical insurance, 155
Medina, 56
Mediterranean holidays, 55
Mediterranean Sea, 33
Meet the Dutch Trade, 174
Mennonites, 162

Mersey Conference Bureau, 168, 174,
    179–181, 180
The Mersey Partnership, 168–169, 173
Mersey Tourism
  Accommodation Call Centre, 171, 173
  advertising by, 169
  BeatleGuides, 173
  and business tourism, 179–181
  conferences with, 174
  events in Merseyside, 181–182
  festivals in Merseyside, 181–182
  information services of, 173
  and leisure travel services, 181–183
  and Liverpool's European Capital of Culture
    bid, 183
  marketing and promotion in, 169–171,
    173–174
  The Mersey Partnership, 168
  MerseyGuides, 173
  at overseas events, 174
  and promotional campaigns, 170
  publications from, 169
  quality control by, 175–176, 178
  research by, 170–171
  and specialist customer service package,
    179–181
  staff training by, 175
  statistics from, 174–175
  target markets of, 173–174
  Tourist Information Centres in, 171, 172, 173
  trade exhibitions with, 174
  Travel Trade Guide by, 181
  visitor surveys by, 174–175
  at World Travel Market, 174
Mersey Tourism Awards, 175–176
MerseyGuides, 173
Merseyside
  digest of tourism in, 171
  events in, 181–182
  expected growth in tourism, 182–183
  festivals in, 181–182
  product themes for, 182–183
  see also Liverpool
Middle East, 27
  see also Dubai
MISTIC reservation system, 173
mobility problems, 75, 76, 148
Monastir, 57
monopolies, 139
monsoons, 40
mosques, 56, 57, 58
motoring requirements, 154

motorways, 116
Mount Vernon, 162
mountain ranges, 33
multiplier effect, 18, 19–20
museum guides, 15
Mustique, 28

national economy, 7
National Statistics, UK, 19
National Tourism Organisations, 12–15
  brochures from, 23
  corporate planning by, 13
  development of tourism by, 13
  and disposable income of tourists, 29
  finance and administration of, 13
  funding of, 13
  marketing by, 13
  research by, 13
  structures of, 165
National Tourist Boards, 14, 55
nationalities of tourists, 29
Nevis, 28
New Prestel, 151
New York, 147, 161
Niagara Falls, 161
niche marketing, 167
nightlife, 182
noise pollution, 22, 110–111
North Pole, 37
North Sea, 33
North West Tourism Awards, 182
North West Tourist Board, 170
numeracy skills, 73

occupancy rates, 102, 171, 175
oceans, 31, 33
Old Town Alexandria, 162
online booking, 73, 74, 150
open jaw tickets, 141
open tickets, 141
organisational image, 119–120
Orient Express, 116
Orlando, 162
over-dependence on tourism, 21
over-development, 22

Pacific Ocean, 33
package holidays, 28
  branding of, 126
  car hire in, 145–146
  charter services for, 109
  on internet, 95
  product differentiation in, 124

short break type, 181
  and tour operators, 7
package products, 91, 95, 136, 137
passport checks, 116
passports, 24, 152–153, 163
payment records, 81, 156
penetration pricing, 127
Pennsylvania, 161–162
people-orientated awards, 176
personal accident, 155
personal possessions insurance, 156
personal skills, 69–70
PEST circle, 121–122
PGL Adventure Holidays, 95
Philippines, 27
place and marketing mix, 129–130
Polar regions, 38
pollution, 22, 110–111
Port Rashid cruise line terminal, 43
ports, 112–113
pre-recorded messages, 152
presentation, 86
preservation of environment, 28
press releases, 131
Preussag, 7
price, 127–129, 140–141
principals, 5, 6, 7–8
  for accommodation, 9
  airlines as, 8, 11
  car hire as, 9
  catering facilities as, 11
  ferry operators as, 8, 11
  incentive commission from, 97
  marketing by, 10
  rail services as, 8, 11
  transport providers as, 5, 8
  and visitor attractions, 11
prior booking, for mobility problems, 148
private developers, 99–100
products
  all-inclusive type, 92
  availability of, 76
  development of, 28
  differentiation of, 124
  homogeneous/heterogeneous types, 88–89
  image of, 119–120
  independent type, 91–92
  inseparable/separable types, 88–89
  knowledge about, 76
  life cycle, 125–126
  in marketing mix, 124–127
  marketing of, 89–91, 93
  multiple type, 99

package type, 91
tangible/intangible type, 88–89
themed type, 182–183
of travel agencies, 91–92, 97
visual attractions as, 90
professional image, 86, 119–120
profit
from accommodation, 102
from customer care, 65, 119
and marketing, 12
and price, 128
promotion
AIDA principle, 132
free offers in, 131
by governments, 23–25
international type, 166
and marketing, 119–123, 131–132, 169–171,
173–174
and marketing mix, 131–132
and presentation, 86
and pricing, 128
and quality, 167
timing of, 132
promotional campaigns, 170
promotional material, 55, 93, 131, 149, 166–167
public relations, 131
public transport, 14, 103–106
publications, 82, 93, 169
Puerto Rico, 28
Punic Wars, 56

quality assurance scheme, 175, 178
quality control, 50, 167, 175–176, 178
quango, 23

rail services, 104, 105–106, 146
rail transport
companies in, 8, 11
cost-effectiveness of, 116
international, 115–116
journey times of, 147
Rashid Al Maktoum, Sheikh Mohammed bin, 44
receipts, 81, 156
recession, 21
records of bookings, 77–79
records of payment, 81, 156
Red Sea, 33
reference sources for travel professionals, 82
regeneration of urban areas, 16
regional tourism, 14, 19, 22
regional tourist boards, 14, 24–25, 93
regulations
for air travel, 110–111

for tourism, 24
for travel, 153
religious values, 16
repatriation costs, 156
repeat business, 65, 71
research, 121, 125, 167, 170–171
reservations, 6, 77–79, 81, 157, 173
central reservations systems, 7, 82
computerised systems in, 6, 73, 81
restaurants, 20
retailers, 94–95, 96–97, 130
revenue, 17
road transport, 116, 147
see also buses
Rome, 105
Ryanair, 140

safari holidays, 39
safety devices for cars, 154
safety of customers, 76
see also health and safety
Saga holidays, 95, 126
St Lucia, 28
St Pete Beach, 162
satellite pictures of Earth, 31
saturation stage in product life cycle, 126
Sbeitla, 56, 57, 58
scheduled services in air transport, 8, 107–108,
138–140
Scottish Tourist Board, 178
sea transport, 112–114
seas, 31, 33
seasonality, 128
secondary research, 121
segmentation of markets, 132
self-catering accommodation, 9, 100–101
on barges, 144
self-drive holidays, 9
see also car hire
sensitivity of tourism, 15–16, 17
Sheraton Hotels, 102
short break packages, 181
shuttle buses, 104, 145
Sidi Bou Said, 56
ski resorts, 40, 53–55
skills shortages, 20
social impacts of tourism, 15–17
socialist countries, 102
sole agency, 97–98
Sousse, 57
South Pole, 37
Spain, 29, 55
special needs, 69, 70, 178

special offers, 128, 131
specialist customer service package, 179–181
spending by tourists, 17, 18
Spirit of Adventure, 95
sports facilities, 16, 28, 44–45
staff
   attitude of, 72–73
   audibility of, 71
   checklists for, 67–68
   and exchange rates, 85
   hierarchy within, 75
   information, 50, 52
   job satisfaction of, 66
   personal appearance of, 72
   and product knowledge, 76
   professional image of, 86
   protection of, 67
   reference sources for, 82
   role in team, 66
   skills for, 69–70, 73
staff training, 7, 24, 64, 175
statistics, government, 121
stopovers, 141
storms, 40
subsidies, 128
sustainable tourism, 167
Switzerland, 53–55, 116
SWOT box, 121–122
Syria, 27

target markets, 123–124, 132, 173–174
tariff details, 82
Tate Gallery, 182
taxis, 104, 145, 147
technological developments, 27, 130
   see also information communicaton technology
technology skills, 73
telephone technique, 69
teletext, 152
temperature, 39
theatres, 11
theme parks, 28
Thomson, 95
Thuburbo Majus, 57
ticket prices, 140–141
time zones, 35–37
timetables, 82, 148, 149
tolls, 116
touch-screen facilities, 14, 151–152
tour directors, 15
tour operators
   and accommodation providers, 137
   booking forms from, 159

brochures from, 7, 39, 92, 131, 148
and customers, 137
direct sell, 7
links with, 135
mass market, 95
and package holidays, 7
role of, 5, 6, 7–8, 94–98
specialist, 95
staff training, 7
trade associations for, 95–96
and transport providers, 137
tourism, 12, 98
   awards in, 175–176, 182
   classifications of, 12
   cultural impacts of, 15—17
   defined, 3–4
   in developing countries, 21
   domestic type, 4
   economic impacts of, 17–21, 164
   employment in, 20–21
   environmental impacts of, 22
   funding of facilities for, 99
   and government, 22, 23–25
   growth of, 25–28
   and host community, 15–17
   incoming/inbound type, 4, 7, 13
   and independent travellers, 9, 28
   international type, 4, 29
   land features for, 33
   leisure type, 4, 5, 12, 42, 103
   and length of stay, 12
   mobility problems in, 75, 76
   nationalities of travellers, 29
   non-domestic type, 72
   outbound type, 5
   overdependence on, 21
   regional type, 14, 19, 22
   sensitivity of, 15–16, 17
   services for, 89–91
   social impacts of, 15–17
   spending in, 17
   studies of, 175
   sustainable type, 167
   transport choices of, 8–9
   trends in, 28
   visitor numbers in, 121, 171, 175
   water features for, 33
   and World Tourism Organisation, 25–28
   see also business tourism
Tourism Concern, 22
tourist boards, 150
   national type, 14, 55
   regional type, 14, 24–25, 93

Tourist Information Centres
  on accommodation, 14
  benchmarking by, 171
  customers of, 75, 171, 175
  electronic communication at, 151–152
  function of, 14–15
  literature for, 93
  location of, 14
  in Mersey Tourism, 171, 172, 173
  promotional material from, 149
  and regional tourist boards, 25
  visitor attraction leaflets in, 150
tourist information services, 24
trade associations, 95–96
trade exhibitions, 174, 178
trade fairs, 23, 93, 178, 181
traditional crafts, 57
traditional industries, 17
trans-continental rail routes, 115
Trans-Siberian Express, 115
transfer services, 145
transit passengers, 141
transport
  and accessibility, 28, 129, 147
  links with, 129
transport providers, 8, 131, 135–137, 148
travel agencies, 91–93
  additional services from, 98–100
  advertising by, 6
  aims of, 6
  bookings by, 6
  brochures in, 6, 148
  for business tourism, 5, 6–7
  commission for, 130
  currency exchange facilities at, 154
  and customers, 159
  and global distribution systems, 151
  itineraries by, 160
  manuals in, 149
  products of, 91–92, 97
  as retailers, 94–95, 96–97
  role of, 94–98
  services of, 91, 97
  sole agency type, 97–98
travel and transport, 89
travel arrangements, 160
travel insurance, 97, 155–156
travel permits, 153
travel regulations, 153
The Travel Service, 136
travel service providers, 5, 6, 152, 181–183
travel trade fairs, 23

travellers, 137, 156
  see also customers
travellers' cheques, 75, 93, 154, 155
tropics, 38, 40
Tunisia, 55–58
Turkey, 99

UK
  Gross Domestic Product of, 18
  National Statistics, 19
  and nationalities of tourists, 29
  spending by tourists, 17, 18
  tourists in Dubai, 44

underground rail network, 104, 146
United Nations, 3
United Nations Development Programme, 99
USA
  air travel in, 34–35, 107
  airlines, 107
  airports, 107
  Cosmos tours in, 141
  itineraries, 161–162
  rail routes in, 116
  tourism in, 29
  transit passengers in, 141
  travellers' cheques in, 154
USSR (former), 27
Uzbekistan, 27

vaccinations, 153, 163
vertical integration, 94
Vietnam, 27
viewdata systems, 6, 151
Villars-sur-Ollon, 53–55
visa requirements, 24, 116, 153, 163
visiting friends and relations, 4, 5
visitor attractions
  attendance numbers of, 171
  catering facilities in, 11
  as destination, 99
  of Dubai, 42
  examples, 11
  and government, 24
  of Hong Kong, 61
  leaflets about, 150
  natural, 42
  of newly developing countries, 11–12
  and principals, 11
  products of, 90
  quality assurance scheme for, 178
  services for, 90

visitor numbers, 121, 171, 175
visitor surveys, 41, 174–175
visitors with disabilities, 148, 178
Voyages Jules Verne, 95

walking guides, 15
water features, 33
water supply, 22
watersports, 42, 44
websites, 25, 73, 86, 169, 175
'What's on' guides, 82
wholesalers, 7, 94, 130
winter sun holidays, 40
Wirral Tourism Awards for Excellence, 176

word of mouth recommendations, 66
work force, 129
    see also staff
World Tourism Organization, 3–4, 25–28, 99, 100
World Travel and Tourism Council, 18
World Travel Market, 174
Worldspan, 151

youth exchange programmes, 16

Zaire, 39
Zama, 56
Zimbabwe, 27
Zitouna Mosque, 56